FROM INCARCERATION TO INCORPORATION

Is dedicated to the millions of men and women who are, have been or may find themselves incarcerated one day.

Life is filled with challenges. Face your challenges with the strength and courage to do better and be better.

Believe in yourself.

No one can't stop you but you.

JM and Randy

© 2009 by Randy Kearse and JM Benjamin. All rights reserved. No part of this book may be reproduced, stored in a retrieval system, or transmitted by any means, electronic, mechanical, photocopying, recording, or otherwise, without written permission from the authors.

FROM

INCARCERATION TO INCORPORATION

The Rise, Fall, and Rise Again of
JM Benjamin

4 FROM INCARCERATION 2 INCORPORATION

Like Minds Come Together

They say your friends are those who know all there is to know about you and are still your friends. Since I was a kid I never really had many real friends and I was content with that. I was never one to be a people pleaser and never got caught up in what one thought about me. Generally people either liked me or didn't, there was never a in between, especially when I began selling drugs. In the streets, my own hood, and even amongst my peers it was that way, so prison was no different. Through-out my incarceration I came across many good brothers' from around the world who had like myself at some point in their lives had gotten caught up in the negativity that eventually landed them in prison. Through my travels I had acquired many associates that had possessed similar characteristics and shared some of my same views, but there had not been many who had made such an impact on me that I befriended them with the intentions of our relationship extending outside prison walls. In 2005, I was transferred to the east side of Fort Dix federal prison. As fate would have it, it was there I had the opportunity and pleasure of meeting someone who would later become not only a colleague but also a friend, author Randy Kearse. In prison, news travels fast, both good and bad. Reading is a great past time for many incarcerated and because word in the facility had been circulating about my talent for writing I came in contact with lots of brothers who were either readers or aspiring writers themselves. One day while at work (barbershop) a fellow inmate, friend, and New Jersey native by the name of Ali Hall told me he wanted me to meet this "good brother" by the name of Moe. He went on to say how the brother was a writer himself and maybe the two of us could link up and come together on something. Ali was like the Mayor of the compound and was someone who I conversed with on a regular basis so he knew how much I enjoyed talking about books and meeting fellow writers. When he told me what housing unit Moe resided as soon as I got off work I sought this brother out just to introduce myself. Needless to say, no one had ever heard of this brother who lived in this particular building. After being unsuccessful with locating Moe I went back to Ali. The next day Ali told me to meet him at the building where he introduced Moe and I. Moe, who I later found out real name was Randy Kearse, in fact did live in the building and had been a resident of the building for nearly five years. That alone spoke volumes what type of brother Moe was. In prison, if one is able to go un-detected or un-noticed in that type of setting majority of the times he/she is someone who focuses on doing their time and not letting the time do them. The first time Moe and I met instantly our vibe was one in the same. Although writing was the basis of our conversation it was not the extent. We spoke about the people and things that were most important to us and what our future plans and goals were upon release. I remember the first time he and I met up and walked the prison track for hours just building. We had been so caught up mentally and intellectually vibing outside prison walls that we hadn't noticed it was time to return to our assigned housing units. After that day we met up faithfully to walk the track and politic about how we would connect on the streets and come together with our work. One evening Moe had made a comment to me after listening to me share my latest thoughts on an idea I had on how I was going to become a successful author. His comment was one that contributed to the solidification of our friendship. "Yo, kid you gonna blow up when you get out, jokers are going to hear you on the radio and read about you in magazines, just take a brother with you when you reach the top." It was not so much as to what Moe had said but how he had said it. His words were encouraging, inspiring, and motivating, not to mention genuine. In a world where there is so much hating going on, especially amongst black men, and black men who come from the streets, his words defined his character that day. The evening before his release, another inmate and I prepared a meal for him and the two of us spoke about connecting in the free world. Many inmates speak about getting out and staying in-touch with someone who they've served time with and there are some cases where some do incorporate there talk into existence while many do not. There was no doubt in my mind that this brother and I's bond would spill over into the free world. I was not surprised when my mother told me that someone by the name of Randy had called trying to get in-touch with me. At the time, I still had a little under a year remaining. Randy had been home for a few months. When I called the number he had left for me I could hear the love in his tone when he expressed how good it was to be hearing from me. We talked almost every day until I was released. We became a part of each other's support system. In the midst of our phone conversation Randy would speak about his project "Changin' Your Game Plan" he wanted to put together for ex-offenders and loved ones of ex-offenders. I remember him speaking about it when we'd use to walk the track. The more he spoke about it the more I tried to encourage him to put it together. I wanted him to know that I believed in him just as much as he'd believed in me. One particular phone call Randy had told me I'd inspired him to call himself to task and offered me an opportunity to be a part of the project. That evening I began to work on my part and contributed my journey of change to Randy's second published work. When I was released I took off running full- speed with my writing career. Randy and I teamed up and began touring with our books all over the world, pushing new products to our people. Thereafter, Randy and I started doing speaking engagements together sharing our journey's of change from institutions, churches, on down to schools. When we're at events or functions together I listen to my friend and colleague speak and in my mind I say, "Man, that's what I was going to say or that's what I was thinking, or I agree one hundred percent," and it takes me back to our friendship of how like minds came together. Randy and I have proven and continue to prove that two people can come together in a negative setting and plan to come together outside prison walls to do something positive. The words Randy had spoken on the track back in 2005 rang true. Since then I have honored his request. Where ever I have gone Randy has always been welcomed and he offers the same in return to me. This book is a commemoration to Randy and I for all the countless of laps we walked around Fort Dix federal prison track discussing what would intended to do in order for us to live better lives and not return back to prison upon our releases.

From Incarceration to Incorporation

By no means am I attempting to use this book to justify my past wrongs, doings and negative behavior. I'm only offering up an explanation and education, for those who don't come from or don't understand the environment I grew up in, but also for those who do. It's my hope that my story and journey of change can be and will be a deterrence and derailment to those who may have similar thoughts or are being exposed to similar situations like mines. As I share my journey with you I hope to inspire and motivate those who may have traveled down or are still traveling down these same dangerous roads but are now looking for some form of relief, guidance or assistance in finding their way back. What I am about to share with you is my reality; my past, present, and intended future.

This book From Incarceration 2 Incorporation is an in-depth read that entails how my colleague and friend author Randy Kearse and I survived dangerous and unhealthy lifestyles and was able to successfully overcome incarceration both physically and mentally through hard work and dedication. By incorporating all the life's lesson we'd acquired on the streets and while in prison, when we re-entered back into society we were prepared to re-write the statistic that says a Blackman coming home from prison is destined to fail. We are living proofs that with faith, hope, will power, education, and most importantly wanting to change for the better, it can be done. If we can do it so can you.

Sincerely,

J.M. Benjamin

About the Author (The Life Of a Hustler)

Allow me to introduce you to whom I believe to be one of the hardest working hustlers in urban lit…

My name is J.M. Benjamin, I am an Award Winning and Essence Best Selling author hailing from out of Plainfield, New Jersey. In 2006, I was released from prison and quickly emerged in the fast growing genre of Urban Literature, making my presence felt with my freshman novel Down In The Dirty, published by Flowers In Bloom Publishing.

Ironically, having spent more than half my life in the streets and a substantial amount of time incarcerated, my only credential as a street tale story teller is simply my own firsthand experience and knowledge of what the streets consist of. My up-bringing provide me with the necessary tools I now utilize in my work. By incorporating what I'm so intimately familiar with into my work, I'm able capture and display the reality and horrors of the streets world-wide.

I became a motivational speaker after numerous articles were featured on my life and the extraordinary journey of an ex-drug dealer and ex-inmate turned author, business owner and asset to his community. I share my many experiences and knowledge of the streets at various high and junior schools, colleges, probation and religious programs for the youth. I go to correctional institutions for incarcerated men and women, and visit urban communities throughout the country as a way of giving back to the community and in turn doing what I can do to make a difference.

My accomplishments as an author have been recognized in The New York Times, The Courier News, The Herald News, NJN News, and in many other media outlets. JOLIE magazine ranked my freshman novel Down in The Dirty as #2 hottest summer read of 2006. I was nominated for Best New Breakout Author of the Year and Best Street Novel of the Year 2006 by the African American Literary Awards, which, I won for Best Street fiction of the Year. I was nominated in two categories and won for Best Street Lit at the Chicago Black Authors & Books Award hosted by Infini Promoters. My title Down in The Dirty was featured on the Wendy Williams Experience Book club as the book of the month for July 2006 and was voted the #1 Urban Book out of the Top 10 Street Lit novels sponsored by The Writer's Inn. All of this was accomplished under a years' time after being released from federal prison.

In Feb. 2007, I self-published my sophomore novel titled My Manz And'Em independently under Real Edutainment Publishing, which I am founder and co-owner of. I was nominated for Best Street Fiction again at The AALA for my second novel. In September of 2007, I partnered up with a friend and opened a music and book store, where my third novel, an Essence Best Seller (May 08) and Black Expression (April 08) favorite, Ride Or Die Chick book release party was held. Six months later my partner and I opened up a larger music and books store downtown in my hometown of Plainfield NJ (144 East Front Street). In October 2007, I ventured out into a another arena of the literary world, trying my hand at street distribution for authors and independent publishers alike, becoming responsible for some of your favorite street lit novels such as Dutch: The Finale, Deadly Reigns: The Next Generation, The Harlem Godfather, and Ski Mask Way, just to name a few, gracing the tables and stores of your local street vendors and African American book stores.

Ultimately, my consistent and quality work ethics landed me an opportunity to become a part of a new distribution company, Alliance Book Group (www.alliancebookgroup.com) where I am now responsible for stores world-wide carrying some of the latest titles by African American authors. I recently launched a yet another new independent publishing company myself, signing new and known authors to A New Quality Publishing, releasing the novel Back Stabbers by my first signed author Nyema Dec 2008. My fourth novel, titled On The Run With Love was released independently under my own company on July 4, 2008.

In addition to From Incarceration to Incorporation, I have two more upcoming novels due to be released 08-09, Heaven & Earth, under my company A New Quality Publishing, and Ride Or Die Chick 2 under Flowers In Bloom Publishing. All of these accomplishments were within a two year time span of my release from prison. From the time I wake up in the morning, until the time I steal a mere three to four hours rest, my day consists of hustling. My new mantra is, "I gotta new product, and I can push it to the whole world without going to prison."

The Courier News Front Page: November 2006
Ex-Plainfield Drug Dealer Earning Kudos as Author
By Bernice Paglia/ Editor

Now Out of Prison: J.M. Benjamin Finds Success In Fiction

Plainfield- J. M. Benjamin grew up during the crack epidemic of the 1980's and became one of stereotypes-a kid running the streets of the West End, fatherless and beyond control of the mother and grandmother who was trying to raise him. "It was like the movie New Jack City when I was growing up," Benjamin said. "Each block had 10 or 12 guys getting a lot of money." But the price of participating in the drug trade then now tends to be either death or imprisonment. In all, Benjamin served six years and three months in state prison and five years eight months in federal prison, all on drug charges, including trafficking, possession, and racketeering. He got out of jail earlier this year, with a new direction and new career. "I realized I had a talent in writing," Benjamin said. "Writing became an outlet." Through hard work and dedication, he said, Benjamin became a published author and recently won a literary award for his novel "Down In The Dirty", a tale of four women who victimized male hustlers until love derails the scheme.

"The reaction from everyone has just been phenomenal," he said. Benjamin now does motivational work with young people in his old neighborhood and said it is an honor to be well regarded now by "the same elders that called the police on me." In tradition of writing what one knows, Benjamin's chosen genre is street fiction, or urban fiction. Its literary patriarchs are Iceberg Slim, who wrote about life as a pimp, and Donald Goines, a chronicler of addiction, crime, and hustling. Some urban fiction reading lists include better-known writers such as Claude Mc Kay and Ralph Ellison. David Wright, a readers' services librarian with Seattle Public Library, described the genre's draw and reasons why librarians should take heed of its popularity in a July Library Journal on-line article. Wright called it, "one of the hottest literary phenomena of recent years," and said it is creating, "huge numbers of new readers," with the side effect of promoting literacy.

At this year's African American Literary Award Show, Benjamin was a finalist in the Break-Out Author Of The Year category and winner of the Best Street Fiction Award. Readers at large nominated their favorites in many categories, putting Benjamin in the company of other winners including Tavis Smiley, Maya Angelou, Walter Mosley, and Tyler Perry. The event was held Sept. 27 at the Alhambra Ballroom in Harlem.

In the 2006 awards, Benjamin's "Down In The Dirty" edged out one of David Wright's "Street Lit Sampler" author, Nikki Turner, who wrote on a similar theme in "Riding Dirty on I-95." Back in Plainfield since July, Benjamin encounters both friends and foes in a new perspective. Once a combatant with police, he said officers such as Andre Crawford now hail his changed life. "It's always good and always a blessing to see someone turn their lives around from a negative to a positive," said Crawford, who is president of Police Benevolent Association Local 19. Instead of having physical confrontation with Benjamin, Crawford now hears Benjamin giving radio interviews about his book, he said. Although some say so-called "gangsta" lit glamorizes the thug life, Crawford said, "They've lived that life at one time. Who better to write a book on how they lived and evolved and came out of it?"

Now Benjamin days are full of book signings, interviews and impromptu sales wherever urban fiction fans gathered. His new goal is to make a transition into "more of a contemporary and motivational author," he said. He wants to write real life stories of people he knew growing up, including the struggle of a mother overcoming addiction and the aspirations of a city boxer who are still his friends. Most of all, he takes pride in his new life, where writing is his first and only job.

"I'm a poster child for change," he said.

16 FROM INCARCERATION 2 INCORPORATION

Author found vision, voice in prison

Sunday, March 25, 2007
By ASHLEY KINDERGAN
HERALD NEWS

PATERSON -- J.M. Benjamin grew up in a housing project in Plainfield, started selling drugs at 12 and served a total of 12 years in prison on drug charges. But before all of that, Benjamin wrote poems. Writing would turn his life around. Today, he makes his living – a modest one, he admits – as an author in the growing genre of urban fiction. Benjamin said he started writing seriously when a prison counselor encouraged him to keep a journal to vent some of the anger that she felt was causing his fights with other inmates. By the time he was released, Benjamin had published a book called "Down in The Dirty," which would go on to win the 2006 African-American Literary Award for Street Fiction. Benjamin signed copies of his latest book, "My Manz and 'Em, at Nu-Xpressions bookstore on Saturday. Several passersby listened to him explain his message – that young men and women in urban environments can do better than running the streets. In Plainfield, he speaks to community and youth groups about his experiences. "I was always good with words," he said. "In the streets, you hide your positive talents and glamorize your negative talents." Benjamin's work is a part of the fast-growing genre of urban fiction. "My Manz and 'Em" is inspired by his own experience, and tells the story of a young man named Malik who goes to prison and struggles not to get dragged back into his old lifestyle when he gets out. But Benjamin isn't trying to glamorize a life of crime. "In my books, the bad guy never gets away," he said. "Because I never got away." Bryan Watson, of South Hackensack, picked up Benjamin's book while shopping with his family Saturday. "I like to support brothers who are putting books out there," he said. "He has a real positive message." Darryl Harris, owner of Nu-Xpressions Gift Shop/Art Gallery, said he invited Benjamin because he thought his experiences might inspire those who had lost hope of turning their lives around. "It's a good example for someone who may be going the wrong way that they can do something with their lives after being in prison," he said. "It took him sitting down in prison and finding out that he had a knack for writing." Benjamin has worked hard to push his book, attending book signings up and down the East Coast and speaking wherever he is invited. His next hope, he said, is to open a black bookstore of his own in Plainfield and make it a literary hangout for a generation of urban youth. Most of all, though, he wants to leave his mark on the urban fiction genre. "Who says because you made a bad decision, you're a bad person or a dumb?"

Ex-Con Back in the 'Hood, Hustling His Novel Now
Dith Pran/The New York Times

J. M. Benjamin found his writing talent in prison.
By KEVIN COYNE

Published: November 25, 2007
Plainfield
Skip to next paragraphIn the Region
Long Island, Westchester, Connecticut and New Jersey

J. M. BENJAMIN finally came home the summer before last after a dozen years in prison, and within a day he was back on the streets, hustling again.

His territory used to be the West Second Street projects, and his product was crack cocaine. "I had a name that was larger than life," he said one recent day, stopping to talk to some friends outside his old neighborhood's building 524, the worn, low-rise brick building that was once his home and headquarters. "If you didn't hustle for any of us {friends}, you couldn't hustle around here."

But on that first full day home in July of 2006 he set up business in a different spot, outside a barbershop near the corner of Park Avenue and Front Street, to take advantage of the crowds gathered for the city's Fourth of July parade. He had a new product, too: the novel he wrote in prison.

A car passed No. 524 {building} now, and the driver shouted the question Mr. Benjamin gets asked wherever he goes in the city where he is on his second time around as a local celebrity, this time for better reasons: "When's the next one coming out?"

"Soon," Mr. Benjamin shouted back. "Real soon." Mr. Benjamin, 33, drives a Mercury Villager minivan now, not the tricked-out Honda Accord, Acura Legends, and Audi 4000s he once favored for hauling kilos of cocaine up I-95 from the Carolinas, and he loads it with the cargo that changed his own life, and that he hopes will change others', too: books.

He read his way through his long days in prison: Dean Koontz, John Grisham, James Patterson, anybody who could tell a crisp story. "And my icon, Donald Goines," he said, referring to the late jailhouse author who was a pioneer of the genre that came to be known as street literature. At the federal prison at Fort Dix, a counselor suggested that Mr. Benjamin try writing something himself, and 400 pages poured out of him, a memoir he called "Everything's Real in the Field," using the nickname for the city where his family has been deeply and widely rooted for generations. Copies of it circulated among inmates, and he was moved to try writing a street novel like the ones he was reading.

"There was a lot of glorifying and glamorizing the streets, and the bad guys were getting away," he said. "They didn't explain how these characters became these types of individuals. I lived the same type of lifestyle they were writing about, only it wasn't pretty to get there."

He wanted to tell the stories of what it's like when the electricity is shut off because you can't pay the bill, when your mother needs money for diapers for your baby sister, and when you look out the window and you see easy money waiting outside — not using drugs yourself, just selling to those who do. And then what happens when the money comes too fast, buying cars and jewelry, but costing your soul. He wrote a novel in 34 days, "Down in the Dirty," and sent it to a small new publisher in Brooklyn. "I could hear it in his voice, that he was really hungry for this," said Nancey Flowers, whose Flowers in Bloom imprint has published 10 books. She regularly receives queries and manuscripts from inmates, and in January will publish a book by Randy Thompson, an author Mr. Benjamin knew in federal prison at Fort Dix. "All the beautiful minds that are in there, it amazes me."

Mr. Benjamin was still in prison when the book was published, but his brother managed to sell enough copies — making the rounds of beauty salons, clubs and restaurants, and tapping into the wide network of family and friends — to get him some coming-home cash. Because Plainfield had no bookstore, his first signing was at a table he set up outside the Nu-Cuts barbershop. The book won a couple of awards, and he took it on the road, visiting every bookstore that would have him, pushing it into a third printing, up to 15,000 copies.

"I go out there and grind, just like before — I just switched my product," he said. "Because I come from the streets, all the so called gangstas and those in the streets respect me. All the time I did is like credibility, which is stupid, but I have a new credibility now because I made it out."

He set up his own company, Real Edutainment, and earlier this year he published a second novel, "My Manz and 'Em," with a cover photo on the steps of No. 524. His third novel, "Ride or Die Chick," is due out this week from Flowers in Bloom. Sitting in his closet at home are 11 other manuscripts he wrote in prison.

And for this newest book, he won't have to stage his first signing on the sidewalk. In September, Don Benito, of Music N Motion on East Front Street, gave him some display cases and wall racks to fill with books. The sign in the store's front window announces: "Black Books Sold Here."
"We're geared toward the upliftment of the communities we come from because we played such a major part in their

destruction," Mr. Benjamin said, unloading a box of new books at the store that were being delivered by his friend, and fellow inmate-turned-author, Randy Kearse. "Just because we're from the 'hood doesn't mean we have to be subject to what goes on in the 'hood."

He added Mr. Kearse's books to the display case, then checked how many he had left of each of his own. He keeps those on the top row, where nobody can miss them.

Imagine This

When we're children, growing up we're often asked the most important yet unknowingly question of our lives, "What do you want to be when you grow up?"

For some, answers such as police officers, firemen, lawyers, doctors, and politicians, are the first to come to mind, while others answer athletes, actors, and entertainers.

It was a frequent asked question to me as a child, a question that would always send my young mind into roam. I would imagine what it would be like for a kid like me when I got older, coming from a dysfunctional home, and was growing up in a poverty stricken environment. We as children, our minds are somewhat like sponges and our lives are similar to a piece of paper. We soak up any and everything we come in contact with, whether visually or something we hear, each time someone crosses our path a mark is left upon us. So between what is taught and told to us in the school system, what is seen on television and the movie screen, what is heard on the radio, and what we are exposed to in the inner city communities we grow up in, we have a tendency of taking what we've absorbed and referencing back to that paper to determine what we feel best suits us and our lives once we reach adulthood, then begin to work towards what we want to become.

24 FROM INCARCERATION 2 INCORPORATION

I too use to imagine being some of those same people I thought to be successful, positive, and productive in society, from the attorney's and physicians down to the athletes and entertainers. I imagined myself making my way through high school, watching my mother proudly in the stands as I accepted my diploma. I imagined furthering my education and finding a high paying job or career. I imagined finding that special someone to build with and spend the rest of my life with. I imagined becoming a father wanting to provide better and more then what I had as a child.

I think I just about imagined the same things the average kid may have regardless to their race, gender, or what part of the continent they resided. But those images and thoughts became wishful thinking for me the day I chose to rush my aging process, thinking I fully understood exactly what I was being exposed to at a young age.

Never in a million years would I have thought that out of all the things in the world I imagined I could be, wanted to be, and had the potential to be, I would have become something I knew nothing about. I never imagined that I would have taken the path I chose to travel down, a path that I later on had to find out the hard way that it was one of destruction. I never imagined that very same path would ultimately end at a brick wall I would eventually find myself on the other side of for a total of a dozen years of my young adult life.

What I once imagined as a child did not become my reality... This is my reality... Imagine this.

They say that we are products of our environments and for many years I use to believe that to be true, up until the time I made a conscious decision to want better for myself and began to work towards that direction while incarcerated. You see, my environment was and still is full of drugs, violence, mayhem, etc, and unbeknownst to me I became a product of just that. Why? Because it was all around me, and I once thought that this was all I knew. For as long as I can remember negative and criminal behavior was displayed in my presence, either in my home or when I walked out the front door. My father was a drug dealer amongst other things. Up until recently, the only memories I did have of my father were of him running the streets and going in and out of prison. For most of my childhood he was incarcerated more than he was home.

Again, I look for no excuses or offer no blame, but as most of us know now, growing up without a strong father in the home or actively involved in our lives puts us at a disadvantage at an early age. No matter how much a mother loves her son(s), no matter how much she tries to teach him how to be a man, or no matter how much she tries to protects them, it's still not the same as having a father in a son's life. Without that much needed guidance a father is supposed to give his son, the son goes through young adulthood trying to find his way alone, easily influenced by that in which surrounds him.

We don't realize how much we're affected by not having a father or a male role model, for that matter, around while we're young until we're men and fathers ourselves. When I was young and I didn't know any better, and though my father played a fleeting role in my life, I still wanted to be just like him. Can you imagine as a kid, you're constantly being reminded by adults of how much you look like this person and how instant respect and admiration is extended to you by those within the community who seemed to have it all, just because of who your father is?

Psychologically that does something to a child. Despite being a smart and talented kid with a promising future, I was impacted by the negative lifestyle and status that my father possessed in our community. Whether intentionally or unintentionally, he contributed to the choices and options presented to me when I was a kid. Can you imagine what it does to a child when they see their parent(s) possess a weapon, commit a violent act, indulge in drug usage/sales, etc?

I remember the first time I had an up-close and personal encounter with drugs. Picture being an eleven years old child watching your father from afar getting high, then he becomes so paranoid from the drug that he places you and another sibling into a bathroom with a substantial amount of narcotics, where you're instructed to shove theses drugs deep into the toilet and dispose of them if you hear a knock on the door. I clearly remember what I was feeling that day as well as the look on my brother's face as if it were happening while I'm sharing this story with you.

A sense of responsibility and power mixed with fear and confusion filled my young body and my brother's facial expression told me that he felt the same inside. I remember

us being amazed at the quantity of drugs in the large zip-lock bag, wondering the value of the package. We had saw similar pictures of drugs on television and in movies and even empty vials scattered throughout the neighborhood but we had never been in possession of drugs, nor did we intend to be.

I can't say this incident was the turning point of my life as far as the path I would take a year later but it definitely played a significant part in my decision making. The saddest thing about that day is that twenty-three years later, me and my father (who has also changed and turned his life around for the better) were having a conversation about where we came from, what we had gone through, and where we were today, and in the midst of the conversation I reflected back to that particular day in the bathroom. Needless to say, my father had no recollection of the incident. I found that to be crazy.

Here it was, my father had done something so detrimental to me and my psyche in the past that it impacted and influenced me negatively as a child and he was totally oblivious to the damage placing me in the bathroom that day had done. I was sure that being a changed man himself that the bathroom incident would be one of the things he regretted doing.

That just goes to show you when someone is so caught up in the streets and indulging in negative behavior he/she will do things in the heat of the moment as a means of survival or financial gain, not realizing or even caring who is watching or who is affected by their actions. There was only one time that I can actually recall my father trying to step up to the plate to be the man I needed him to be after he had just been released from prison.

I can remember him standing in front of my brother and me in our apartment saying, "Listen, I have been hearing about you two all throughout the system (prison). Everybody's talking about my sons got it going on out here. And I blame myself for not being here for you so you wouldn't have to go this route, but I'm here now and all this nonsense is about to come to an end."

By that time it was already too late because the damage had long ago been done and my brother and I was already knee deep in the game, practically seasoned veterans. I didn't say anything, but I was in agreement with my brother's response. "Where were you when our moms were out here struggling? Huh? He questioned my father. "Don't try to come home and no father now, it's too late for that," he added.

At the time, like my brother had stated, my father was fourteen years too late for me and sixteen years too late for my brother to try to come and dictate what we could and couldn't do. Knowing what I know now, I have to respect my father for his attempt to reach out and try to save his sons from the lifestyle that had basically destroyed his life and kept him away from his family for so many years. As I was going through my process of change, I couldn't help but to think back to that day and wonder what had transpired between me, my brother, and our father, that day in our apartment when he came to save us. As a man, what had it done to him just coming home from prison, wanting to put his family back together?

Not too long after, my father had fallen back into his old criminal behavior. If I was asked why I think he resorted back to a life a crime, I would have to answer, "One, because he couldn't cope with failure, he had no backup plan to back up the plan he had planned to incorporate into society before he was released. Two, he had no real strong support system that he could turn to or was willing to turn to, and Three, he simply went back to what he felt was all that he knew, his comfort zone where he knew he'd be embraced and welcomed with opened arms. These are the main reasons why so many of our men and women return back to the streets and to a life of crime, and these are the main reasons why the recidivism rate for returning back to prison is so high.

My father admitted to my brother and me later on in life that the confrontation and the words that were said to him that day at our apartment cut him deeply and hurt him a way he had never been hurt before. Being a father myself I often feared my own children having similar words for me prior to coming home. My son was born while I was in prison and my daughters were mere babies when I went away. My children are now thirteen, fourteen, and fifteen, one boy two girls. Between state and federal, I gave the system over twelve years of my life, I have been home nearly three, you do the math and you'll understand my fear. Many of you may possess this same fear. I forced my children to grow up without a father in their lives and it shames me. It was partially because of that reason I decided to work on bettering myself while confined, using them as motivational fuel for my vehicle of change.

Sometimes we cannot find something within ourselves to want to change or work towards change and want better, so we have to find something else to inspire, motivate, or encourage us to begin the process. Most of us are parents and we have to understand the mental, emotional, and psychological damage we cause our children by not being out here with them, especially when it comes to our daughters. For us men, a father is the first man a daughter forms a bond with and without that bond a lot of times a daughter goes astray in many different ways then boys do. Females sometimes subconsciously chose a male who she relates to her father.

For me, being blessed with two daughters was a gift and a curse. I knew it would kill me to have my daughters choose someone similar to how I was in the streets so I knew I had to and was determined to become a man that I would appreciate them choosing if they related him to me. For the mothers who are incarcerated, it goes deeper. When I was serving my prison sentence, it was my mother who served day for day with me. We don't realize when we put ourselves in position that find us imprisoned we take with us those who love us unconditionally. I took my mother. Reality set in as time went by. My mother would always say to me, "A hard head makes a soft bottom." It wasn't until I went to prison that I learned the depths of her words.

All the so-called friends I had —all the women who professed to love me etc, it was my moms who saw to it that her phone was always on to accept my expensive collect calls. It was my moms who sent money from what little she had. It was my mom who saw to it that I received pictures of our family, and it was my moms who came to visit and occasional bring my children despite the fact she lived in Illinois and my children lived in New Jersey. And it was mom who visited me whatever state I was shipped to.

This is yet another element that contributed to my journey of change and my wanting to take advantage of the time I was serving in prison, using it both as a growing and learning experience to prepare myself for when I was released. As a man who went to prison at a young age, I would always wonder each time I saw my mother's face on visit, year in year out, watching her hair go from jet black, to salt and pepper, and then a full set of shinny silver, "Could I or would I have been strong enough to ride for my moms the way she so diligently rode and continues to ride for me unconditionally?" Right, wrong, or indifferent, my mother has been there for me and I couldn't imagine life without her being there.

I frequently visit female correctional facilities and speak to the women serving time in these cold and desolate places and it saddens me because when I see the faces of the women sitting in those chairs, I see my sisters, aunts, cousins, daughters, and mother. I think about all of the children who were already fatherless, now motherless. I think about all the men who just needed that strong and good woman beside them. And then I think about all of the women who are sitting in those seats behind loving the wrong man. During my speech I ask these women two very important yet emotional questions, "One, is the man or the streets you so loved and ran holding you down the way you would have or have held them down? And two, who's holding your children down while you're away?"

They say never judge a person unless you've walked in their shoes and I've found that statement to be all so true. From summer 2008-winter 2008 one of my daughters had to come live with me. Although I was grateful and blessed to be in a position to provide a roof over her head, in that short period of time I received a crash course on what it was like and had been like for her mother in my absence to take on the role of both parents. Needless to say, I gained more respect then I already had for my daughter's mom because it was hands down a difficult transition and adjustment for me to make being someone used to living alone and not have a full time responsibility such as a child, let alone a young growing female teen to tend to.

My point, you women are indeed the back bones and foundations of families. No one can do your jobs, as women- as mothers better then you. Your presence is greatly missed and well needed. It is my opinion that your absence in the real world in the children's lives contributes to the increasingly demise and destruction of our youth. If you don't have the power to change for self, please, I encourage you to think about the babies. In majority of cases, it is the mother who is abandoned with child/children and is forced to fend for self and family.

As a single parent, my mother bent over backwards working multiple jobs and trying to further her education to provide the best life she could for me and my siblings in the absence of my father. She always saw to it that we knew there was life outside the ghetto. She instilled in us all morals, respect and all other qualities a child should possess, but there was no way my mother could be there to hold my hand twenty-four hours a day seven days a week and still provide for me or my siblings with the basic necessities. Despite all the necessary tools and ammunition my mother armed me with and all the preaching and teaching she gave me to in order to fend for myself in her absence, I simply chose the latter.

****

For acceptance from my peers I made bad choices and poor decisions and because of that I had to deal with the consequences and repercussions behind making them. Because of my reckless behavior and the irresponsible situations I put myself in; I spent many years of my life incarcerated. During my incarceration I tried to repair the damage I had done to myself and tried to minimize, if not cease the pain I had caused my family.

Like so many, I used to spread chaos and mayhem within my community and wherever else I traveled through drugs and violence. But notice how I said "used to", because today, I can honestly say that after my incarceration I chose not to live that type of way any longer. I am a changed man- a different man today then I was back then. I'm not going to pretend that it was an easy or simple journey to reach where I am in life today because I would lying to you, but nevertheless it was and still is a journey worth taking.

They say the best things in life are the ones in which you work the hardest for. Each day I wake to start my day is a process; when I start it, I focus on that day and that day alone. I believe in one step at a time because I know I'm only one bad choice or decision away from returning back to prison and calling it my new permanent place of residency. So I focus on making the best choice and decision for that day, just day, never forgetting where I came from and how I got there.

When I started hustling, there was no overnight or instant success; it all came with time and dedication to the negativity I indulged in so I'd be foolish or irrational to expect for things to change in my life so rapidly. Nothing in life comes easy and change is probably the hardest mission for anyone to partake in, but it's doable. Everything Is A Process! Now all I do is apply the same energy I once applied into something negative into something positive.

Young Eyes

Looking back, I never really had a childhood or rather I have no real clear recollection of one. In fact, even now as an adult certain things about my childhood or my pre- hustling days a family member, associate, or ex-schoolmate may recall seems foreign to me. During a television interview with NJN on the show Another View with Candace Kelley, Candace mentioned my mother telling her behind the scenes that I had once been a boy scout, then a picture of me in a boy-scout uniform posing with another uniformed kid appeared and flashed across the screen. Needless to say, I did not recall ever being in the boy scouts nor did I recognize the kid who I had posed with in the photo, but if you asked me to play the tape back for you when I first sold drugs, everything in between, up until the last time, I can almost quote it verbatim.

At the young rebellious age of twelve years old I began losing sight of my childhood. Memories of an innocent kid were erased and replaced with information that my young eyes and ears shouldn't have been privy to. It's funny, because when you're young and in the midst of all the chaos and mayhem it seems natural to you, just your everyday living, like you become immune to it.

My friends and I all began to travel down many different paths of destructions around the same time, yet we still met outside to play football, basketball, or any other activities we enjoyed prior to entering the drug trade. Ironically, it was those activities that enabled us to go undetected by the police for so long. We were so young and small that when the narcotics task force rolled up around the projects to run down on the drug dealers they targeted the older hustlers and overlooked the group of kids on the basketball court or huddled up with the football. It wouldn't be until months to years later they discovered that we were actually the ones they should've been targeting along. It was us who had a thousand dollars or more worth of product in our pockets and another thousand or more in cash in our socks.

I'll never forget the first time the cops paid me any attention, which was understandable. Here you have it, a young teenaged kid (fourteen years old at the time) hanging out on the block during school hours, not just one day, but several days repeatedly. What could I possibly be doing out there? Looking back, I should've asked my own self that question, maybe things would have turned out differently, but because I didn't and they did, this would be my indoctrination into the flip slip of hustling.

At the time my brother and I had ventured out from the second street housing projects onto another known drug infested area known as Third Street between the Spooner Ave and Grant Ave section of my town.

Anyway, a police car slowly rolls up on the scene where several dealers are standing. I could see the vehicle had only contained one officer, a female, a white female at that, so I was un-concerned by her routine stop. Like in most cases though, those who were dirty (in possession of contraband; drugs, weapons, etc) began to fade into the background or attempt to inconspicuously walk off in hopes of evading a brush with the law and possibly the system.

I myself remained standing there. You see, even at fourteen years old I thought I was Mr. Untouchable, but the reality was I was just young, wild, and reckless, not to mention stupid, naïve, and ignorant to the law, so I had no respect for it back then. I actually thought I was smarter than they were. I literally thought I could beat the system. In my mind, I rationalized that if I moved then I would appear just as guilty as those who had just slithered off. This rationale would have proved rational but for the fact that I was guilty, I had eighty-three bags of crack cocaine in my right pocket and a few hundred dollars in my left. My theory was working for me for a minute as me and the Caucasian female officer's eyes met. My young ego fueled my arrogance as I even said to myself, "I wish she would get out that car I'll dip on her ass." You see, I had no respect for the law or authority. I was ready to have her give chase if she opened that car door. Ultimately that's exactly what wind up happening.

After playing the staring game with her for a few minutes, hoping she would just pull off and move onto the next drug area, something made me glance down to the ground. I could feel my armpits, palms of my hands, and forehead beginning to perspire as my eyes happened to catch a glimpse of what lay beside me on the ground. As lucky as I thought myself to be Lady Luck was nowhere to be found, had it not been for bad luck I wouldn't have had any at all that day. In the midst of the other dealers stepping off, someone had dropped their product right by my foot. I don't know if she saw it, but I couldn't take that chance. As if on cue, as soon as I made an attempt to walk off her words echoed on the side of my face, "Where you goin' kid?" My reply was, "You talkin' to me?" turning to look back hoping she couldn't notice my new-found nervousness. It was the only thing I could muster up at the time. My heart was beating like a bass-drum in a marching band. It took everything within my will power to maintain external coolness. "Never let'em see you sweat," was the motto for that day and that's what I was trying to do. Her response was, "Yeah you, come here," she ordered right before I saw the back-up patrol car pull up.

Enough was enough.

Seeing back-up was all the confirmation I needed to send me off to the races. I instantly took flight and just like I knew, she gave chase. I was quick when I was younger and full of energy. In rapid speed I made a fast dash like Carl Lewis through a backyard and all in one motion catapulted myself over what I believed to be a ten foot plus fence into someone else's backyard. I knew the area all too well and I knew once I got on to the next street I could make my way back to the housing projects where I was from. I could hear her walkie-talkie in the distance as she screamed and roared into the receiver.

At the time I was only about 5ft tall give or take and she was shorter than me. Plus with all her equipment, I knew she was having a difficult time getting over that fence. As I made my way onto South Second Street I saw a police car. I assumed they were looking for me. The sight of the car forced me to double back into the backyard. It was evident that they were closing in on me, so I did the most logical thing. I hid my package in the backyard. Just as I secured my package and was ready to walk back onto the street as if I had done nothing wrong, out of nowhere I was bum rushed by the officer whose car I had seen. Apparently he had seen me also. He shoved me against the side of the house and began searching me aggressively. "Where's it at?" he questioned. "Where's what?" I replied as I looked over my shoulder. I was good with faces, especially those who were cops because they were good for dressing in regular civilian clothes posing as users or dealers who were looking to purchase product wholesale but I had never seen this officer before. He was African American. All I could think about was how he towered over me, standing at about six-foot three. "Turn around and don't move," he shouted, placing his right leg between my legs and gripping me tightly by the belt loop of my jeans as he proceeded his pat search. Knowing what I know of the law now I realize that my rights had been violated, despite the fact that I was in the wrong.

The officer never bothered to even read me my Miranda rights, but when you're un-educated about something people will capitalize off of your ignorance, and I'm sure he knew that I had no real knowledge of the law whatsoever. As he continued to search me, the female officer finally showed up. "Wham, don't you ever F**kin' run from me you hear me!" she roars punching me in the back of the head. Instinctively, I was that close to turning around and delivering a blow back to her but thought better of it. Here I am in a backyard on the side of a house with two cops and no witnesses, not a good look.

Instantly my youth kicks in as I say, "I didn't do anything." That only fueled her anger. "Don't you f**kin' gimme that shit!" she bellows as she begins to claw at my face. "Don't you ever f**kin' run from me again," she repeats. Her colleague stood and watched as she delivered her assault on me.

Thinking back, I wonder why he allowed such an act. Furthermore what did that say about him as a man? Not only as a black man, but a man who took an oath to protect and serve. That day I needed to be protected. Maybe he could have been that role model or male figure in my life to say, "Young brother this is not the way." I'm not saying I would have listened, but two wrongs definitely don't make a right. That could have very well been the day where I could have taken my last breath. There are so some many cases where young black males aren't fortunate enough to make it out of a run in with the law in hand cuffs, but rather a body bag.

When we're out there hustling we often don't think about the severe consequences and repercussions behind what we're doing until we're either smack dead in the middle of a situation or after the fact.

****

I remember as a youngster, in the days before I started hustling, how this brother by the name of Ralphie "D" was amongst the rankings in my hometown of having a name and reputation in the streets larger than life. He was one out of the many street hustlers my friends and I would look up to and admire. We would imagine being in his shoes when we got older. Every time I saw Ralphie "D" he was wearing the latest fashion gear and the biggest and most expensive looking jewelry it seemed money could buy. One un-eventful evening Ralphie "D" eluded the police by running through the housing projects I was from. I remember being with my brother and some friends hanging out in front of our project building when we saw Ralphie "D" blow right pass us, the sirens wailing in the air thereafter. It wasn't long after seeing Ralphie "D" sprinting through the projects and disappear through the maze of buildings, that we heard the shots ring out.

Later, we found out that Ralphie "D", an urban icon in our neighborhood was gunned down by a police officer in the back of our housing projects. It was later confirmed that Ralphie "D" was unarmed when he was killed, and the official statement was, the glare from his jewelry made the shooting officer assume that he possessed a firearm.

As kids, we didn't fully understand or know what type of lifestyle Ralphie "D" lead or how he came to live in the manner in which he chose. All we knew was that this brother gave us dollars for candy, video games, etc, and that he didn't deserve to lose his life the way he had.

****

After the female officer finished unleashing her sadistic attack on me, a child, all I could think about was the slaying of the late Ralphie "D" Woods and count my blessings. That day contributed to the resentment I had built up towards police. Although I was playing an adults game, I was still a child with a child mentality so it all goes back to us as children being like sponges and pieces of paper.

The drugs I hid were never discovered but I did have three loose bags of crack stuck in between my money, so I was charged with those drugs and the package that lay next to my foot, so I guess she did see the package after all.

Years later the impact of that incident would be the underlying reason which caused me to have several confrontations with the law.

This would be the first time I had ever experienced the feeling of hand-cuffs. The uncomfortableness was overwhelming. Imagine both hands placed behind your back, then being subdued and restrained by metal tightly squeezing up against your flesh, and your wrist bones. The pain and discomfort it offered was excruciating, especially when I was thrown into the back seat of the police car. With each pot hole, bump in the road, corner turned, pressure was applied to my wrist. Tears of pain formed in the creases of my eyes as I huffed and puffed out of frustration and I cursed myself for being in the position I was in.

By the time we arrived at Plainfield police station I was glad to be transported out of the car and into the facility. As I was escorted inside I could see a collage of familiar faces of officers who had patrolled my housing projects and the Third Street area. Comments like, "I knew they were gonna catch you." And, "Where'd you get him at?" "What you bust him with?" While others offered head shakes of disappointment and nods of approval of my capture.

Being the man I am today I understand the science behind both the headshakes of disappointment and nods of approval I received from the cops that day. Having crossed paths with some of these same officers who played a part in taking me off of the streets, I know that the disappointing head shakes were because they hoped or wished that myself and many other young brothers and sisters didn't fall victim to the stereotypes that get us sucked into the system. While the nods of approval were from those who felt the streets would just be a little bit safer with me off them. Honestly, they both were right. I did fall victim to the stereotype and eventually got sucked into the system, and my neighborhood was a little bit safer in my absence because I was a major contributor to the destruction of my community.

I was taken to a back room where I was stripped searched. I remember feeling childlike and embarrassed the first time I was ordered to strip down to the bare nude in front of another male. But after so many juvenile arrests that were to come, I'd become immune to it. Nevertheless, I never got use to the feeling that swept through me each time I had to. It was a very degrading feeling. Later on in life I would find myself in a similar but much more degrading situation as my criminality progressed.

Normally, the police would contact a parent or guardian and released you in their care, but after an hour or so of questioning without receiving the answers they were looking for, they decided to have me transferred to The Union County Detention Center, which was considered a county jail for us juveniles. The ironic thing about their decision to send me to the "Youth House" as it was called, was that I actually welcomed and embraced going there. Even though I really didn't want to be locked up, in the back of my mind I wanted to go to the detention center. In the streets your status is defined by some of the most foolish things in the game; how much drugs you're pushing, how much money you're making, what type of car you drive, what type of jewelry you wear, how fly you dress, how many fights you won, how many people you shot, and the most ignorant one of them all, how much time did you do?

When I was coming up, going to jail or prison was like a stripe or badge of honor, at least that's what it was perceived as. We buy into this façade, because that's all that the streets is, one big illusion that we all chase after, only to find out sooner or later things are not what they always appear to be.

The stories I use to hear about prison and what I use to see when people came home created a perception in my mind that possessed no fear. Had someone come home and told the stories of the rapes, murders, and deaths that occur in prison or even about some of the degrading things you're subjected to while incarcerated maybe that would have deterred me from following down that same path of destruction they had. Instead they would come home and return to the hood fifty to a hundred pounds heavier from working out and eating good while away. They'd come home with a glow and shine that over shadowed those of us who had been hustling and grindin' day in and day out. They would be embraced with opened arms by the entire hood with nothing but love and respect. Females who never paid them any attention before was now lining up to get a moment of this individuals time.

For weeks, sometimes months there would be no need to return back to the block or think to get a job because you were taken on shopping sprees by your most closest comrades, and when you did get back into the game a certain respect was given and some sort of fear was instilled in those who had never experienced prison life because you did a "Bid" and survived. But being someone who has done time both as a juvenile and adult and experience that "Just came home feeling", I can truthfully say that it all boils down to peer pressure. Even if I had wanted to change or want better for myself back then it would have been difficult, having to return right back to my community.

In Narcotics Anonymous and Alcoholic Anonymous they teach and practice changing your surroundings, people, places, and things. An addiction is an addiction and although I was not addicted to drugs or alcohol I was addicted to a criminal lifestyle and behavior so because I did not remove myself from my addiction I did not allow myself the opportunity to want better and do better back then.

When I went to the youth house it was like going off to college after I had gone through the formalities. For the second time that day I was stripped and searched. This time I was ordered to shower and apply a lice and crab shampoo to everybody part that possessed hair, which was my entire body. I was then given a pair of elastic waist blue jeans (nothing like the Lee's and Levi's I was use to) and a tight fitted red T-shirt along with a bed-roll. I could hear someone call out from behind one of the metal doors they were locked behind. "Yo who dat?" And I answered, "Squirm from The Field," proudly giving my street name and town's monarch. By morning, word had spread through-out the small facility like wild-fire that they had "Caught" Squirm from the New Projects.

In my town and various others, at a young age, my brother Pete (Peter Pan) and I names were legendary in the streets. Names we lived for and represented sun up-sun down. Names that were given to us in there purest form by our mother and grandmother and we allowed them to be tainted by the streets and those in them. Names that put us and forced us into positions and situations we now wished we'd never would have been in, again peer- pressure.

When I entered the dayroom area I noticed many of my illegal colleagues I hadn't seen in months and even years were residents of the facility. They too had bought into the system. Years down the line many of those same faces I had come across in adult facilities both state and federal. Even some of the females who traveled in my same circle in the streets resided in the youth jail. You had some of the most notorious young hustlers and gangsta's from Bilal Pretlow's E'Port Posse/ Phazell down to Plainfield's blocks like The Old and The New Projects, Arlington Ave, and Third all piled up in one room, all dressed alike, no big I's and no little U's.

These were some of the same faces that I encountered at The Geek Festival in Philadelphia's Fairmount Park or New Jersey's Belmar, or at The Rink in Bergenfield Teaneck, or then Echoe Lanes bowling alley, or The Amboy movie theatre, or some of the Tri-State area's hottest club, sporting their Gucci, MCM, Polo, Louis Vetton gear and truck jewels, pushing their 318i or 325i BMW, 190E or 300E Benz, Audi 4000s or 5000s, or Jetta's, etc but now here it was all we had were memories, war stories we called them, until we returned back out there to create more.

Eventually, I ended up serving ten days that particular time because on my first appearance after four days before the courts the judge deemed me to be a menace to society and a threat to my community and felt I needed some more time to think about my actions. I remember my mother being in the court room making a failed attempt on my behalf giving the judge her reasons why he should release her son. As tough as I thought myself to be, it almost brought tears to my eyes hearing my mother say, "My son is a good kid, an A-B student," and a lot of other good qualities she felt I possessed. I detected the pain in my mother's voice as she pleaded with the judge to let her baby come home.

Even though they should have been, my mother's words were not enough to convince the judge to let me go. Hearing my mother talk about me like that, made wonder was I was who she said I was. Before they transferred me back over to the youth house they gave my mother and I a few minutes. Her words plunged into my heart like a poisonous spear. "Don't worry, you'll be okay. They'll let you out the next time. God will see to that." On the outside I gave her an affirming smile, but on the inside I was in hurting. Not for myself, but for my mother.

Back then I was not mature enough or knowledgeable enough to realize that I had made her my co-defendant and incarcerated her because whether I wanted her to be there for me or not she was going to be. Despite the dozen or so years I served as an adult in prison, back then those ten days were equivalent to ten years to me. When I was released, you would have thought I had put on the fifty to a hundred pounds I spoke about earlier. The love that I received upon my release blinded me and made me feel that I could do what I was doing forever, prison or not, I was in love with the streets.

As time progressed, my brother and I climbed up the criminal ladder, making even bigger names for ourselves in the streets. Names that were being mentioned in the same breath as some of those who we had idolized, admired, and looked up to when were younger. Our names were ringing like the bells of Sunday Mass. We had literally become neighborhood/street/ghetto celebrities. Due to our dedication and consistent hard work on the block my brother and I names gained a certain status amongst our peers in the streets but with those names came more than we had bargained for we would soon find out.

My tenth grade year of high school I made one of the worse decisions I could have made as a young teenager. My mother wasn't lying when she told the judge I was an A-B student up until the time I traded my school books for drugs. In junior high school it was easier to maintain my education and balance it with the block. In fact, being a student made for a great cover-up during the time my friends and I discovered how to go to the "City", New York City that is, to purchase our own product in bulk.

My seventh and eighth grade year in Maxson junior high school, during my lunch breaks or the early part of school I would skip classes, hop on the train with my book bag full of books headed to New York to cop, blending in with the typical New York kids who were in route to their own schools. The only difference was while they possessed lunch money in their pockets, I possessed drug money in mine. By the time I made my purchase and started to make my way back to New Jersey in hopes of catching my last few class, it would be lunch time for students, and again I would blend right in, only this time I would not only have a book bag containing school books, but enough drugs to make my brother and I thousands of dollars.

Looking back, the danger of what was so normal for me is so overwhelming. During those times it was reported in the media and spoken about in the street how hustlers from various parts of New Jersey and other states were being robbed and murdered in the very same places I was purchasing my drugs from I never entertained the thought nor did it ever dawn on me that that could have easily been me who became a statistic or victim of circumstance.

I remember one day my school had conducted a random locker search, targeting lockers they may have had suspicion of some illegal activities taking place from out of it. They had each class come out into the hall-way and stand by their assigned lockers. As they approached where I stood, I was already preparing for the worse. I just knew they had been tipped off about the package I possessed in the top part of my locker that I had just hours ago placed inside after returning back to school after a trip from The City. "You, open your locker," they demanded, only they were talking to the kid whose locker was next to mine. I'm thinking to myself, they got the wrong locker and the wrong kid because I knew the kid who stood next to me. He didn't come from where I came from nor was he a hustler by far. I was dying with laughter inside until they pulled out a sandwich bag full of white powder and escorted him to the office. I couldn't believe my eyes; it looked as if he'd possessed every bit of four and a half ounces worth of cocaine. Later we had found out that this kid was running around school pretending to be a drug dealer, flashing the so-called product (baking soda) to other students. Here it was, this kid was growing up in a nice neighborhood, had come from a good background, had both parents in the home, and he was pretending to be something that I wish I would have never been exposed to but had become.

Looking back now, I wish I had taken heed to that day that baking soda had been discovered in the kids locker of the seriousness of what I was involved in, but I needed more convincing and I would later get just that. One of the worst decisions I made was when I decided to quit school to run the streets full-time. Even through high school I was an above average student, still getting A's and B's when I dropped out in my 10th grade. The only education I thought I needed from this point on was, a street education, and the blocks that I'd hustle on and lock down would be my school.

My brother quit in the ninth grade. When we were young a whole lot of us chose street smarts over book smarts. And as the saying goes, "had I known what I know

now, I would not have done some of the things that I did." And that's real!

With the decision to abandon my education behind me, each day I learned something new in the streets and about myself, none which was healthy or positive. As a means of survival and protection, I possessed a firearm using it to gain street credibility and respect amongst my peers aswellas invoke fear within my adversaries. I found myself adapting and indulging in the same behavior I had been exposed to by my father, other family members, and other unscrupulous individuals within my community, minus the drug usage. My criminality and violent behavior compensated for the narcotics I chose not to consume. I was just as much addicted to the life style as a fiend was to a crack-cocaine or heroin. I was addicted to the thousands of dollars I made day- in and day- out, I was addicted to the expensive cars I drove, the partying, and the expensive clothes I wore. I was addicted to being in the lime light and having my name travel like that of sound through-out my town and town alike. I was addicted to the women who were attracted to those in my illegal profession. Furthermore I was addicted to the streets.

In my opinion, I believe those of us who had never fallen victim to using narcotics believed that we had more control over what we were doing in the streets and never related it to being an addiction. We often found ourselves saying, "I can stop anytime I want to." If that is the case then why does it take for most of us to go off to prison, not once but two, three, four times, etc, and still we come home and turn back to the thing(s) in which will so easily return us back to a place we despise and know makes us unhappy. The truth is, when we're in the streets, we have no control over ourselves or the streets we profess to love and run. The definition of an addict-is (one who devotes or gives oneself habitually or compulsively to something, to cause to become compulsively or physiologically dependent on the habit forming substance, to become enslaved by.)

I don't know if you are ready to, but I can honestly admit that I was devoted to the drug game, habitually and compulsively. I was physiologically dependent on the money that I made and I was enslaved by the streets and all which pertained to it. Therefore, based on the definition given, I am an Addict. That is something many of us must come to terms with in order to move on in our lives. Admit your addiction in order to overcome it. As time progress, the A's and B's I was so accustomed to receiving in school were now being replaced by lower grades in the school of hard-knocks, as I learned valuable lessons at my own expense the hard way.

Changin' Your Game Plan (For The Worse)

As I mentioned earlier on, my father ultimately resorted back to what he felt he knew best at the time-the streets. Despite the fact that he was not actively involved in my upbringing and was incarcerated more then he was in the free world, still he played a significant part in the way I looked at many things as a child. Ironically, the things I was learning just by watching and listening from him were things I did not want to become but in fact became unintentionally.

When I was a kid, I resented my father for all that he had put my mother and our family through, the verbal, mental, physical, emotional abuse he had put my mother through, and not being there for me and my siblings. I had all of these things built up inside of towards my father, but the day he was released from prison, the same day he made the failed attempt to save my brother and I, was the day all of those feelings went out of the window.

In spite of all of the resentment and animosity that I had built up in me for all those years of abandonment and pain he'd caused to my mother, for some reason I remember being happy to see him after pausing a cee-lo dice game we were having in the hall-way of the building 524 in my housing projects my brother and I grand-parents resided. Maybe because he and I were one in the same at the time, and prior to his release I had walked in some of his same shoes, but now I can say I wear and walk in different pairs of shoes, positive and productive one, as does my father, and my brother.

That day he and I exchanged greetings and manly hugs, father-son, hustler to hustler. Today we exchanged greetings and manly hugs, father-son, man to man, and that's the power of change. After that emotional day between my father, myself, and my brother, my father had disappeared. When he finally did re-surface after coming home from prison, again he sought my brother and I out once again to reason with us, only this time it was not a reasoning that would save his sons, but assist in the destructive path we were already traveling down.

On this particular day I remember a beige pick-up truck with a white camper on the back sporting South Carolina license plate rode pass some friends and I on second street and turned onto the side street of Elmwood Place. Instantly we all sprung into action thinking the vehicle to be that of a paying customer of the product we possessed. Needless to say, it was non other then my father.

I often wish that day I would had never saw the camper ride pass, let alone saw the driver, but because I did I now chalk it up as being the inevitable and a part of my growing and changing process. Back then it was for the worse though. That day my father along with my brother and me again went off to talk. These were my father's words. "You two are gonna keep messin' around nickeling and diming it out here and find yourself in somebody's prison for a long time. Ain't no real money up here anymore. The real money is in the south." At the time I was fifteen years old, my brother turning seventeen. At that age, we were making tens of thousands of dollars in our hometown, more then our young minds knew what to do with it. But something about what my father was saying seemed appealing to me.

My brother was always the cautious one, me, I was always ready to jump at any and every opportunity that presented itself or seemed prosperous, a habit that would later play a significant part in the amount of time I served in prison. Again, my brother was the first to speak, but this time not the only one. "The south, nah we good. I don't anything about no south, I know the projects." Like most of the things my brother had said, I was in agreement. He was right, we didn't know about the south, but I was interested in finding out. All I had to do was roll with what my brother had said and my father probably would have left as he did the first time my brother spoke his peace, but instead I added. "Bro, it sounds like it could be worth looking into. How about you stay up here and I go down with dad and check things out." My brother asked, "Are you sure?" He knew that if there was money to be made his younger brother could make it. He had watched me single handedly out-hustle some of the most money getting individuals around our hood and on another block we had hustled on, young and old alike. So when I answered "yeah." That was enough for us to discuss our plan.

My father said he'd be ready to pull-out in three days. Up until the last second my brother and I went over all we had been discussing about my intended trip. You see in my father's absence, all we had was Us once we chose the streets, so the trust and faith we had in each other we didn't for him. This was my first experience I had with what I now know to be classified in a court of law as drug trafficking, a crime I was charged and convicted of not once, not twice, not three, but four times. Now, ask yourself, when does one say enough is enough. Everyone has there limitation, I had not yet reached mine.

I sat in the back of my father's camper with God knows how much drugs of his and four and a half ounces of crack cocaine, which is one hundred and twenty-six grams, an eighth of a kilogram, known as a "Big Eight. Back then, in my hometown, it's wholesale purchase price would have been $2,250 street valued $5,000 to $6,000, but from what was told to me by my father and I soon found out, it's wholesale purchase price was $8,100 and street valued $19,200. The experience was enough to further corrupt anyone who lived the type of life style I had. When my father pulled into a complex which was considered to be the towns housing projects and I got out of the back of the camper I could see this was where it went down. Its funny how because you come from something you can easily recognize it when you see it, regardless what part of the world you're in.

In spite of how they dressed or the difference in our accents, when I looked and watched them in there small community displaying what I knew they felt to be normal I saw my friends and I. Hundreds of miles of way of we were doing the same exact things. I guess they too recognized that I had come from what they had because they had embraced me with open arms. I was treated like a movie star from Hollywood by both male and female just from the way I dressed and talked. I had a different swag some would say. In total, I was in the south that first time for about four days and during that time all I could remember was partying more then hustling. But on that fourth day when it was time to go back up North, all the product I had transported down was replaced with money.

When I got back home and relayed all that had taken place to my brother, the two of us decided to pack up and take our show on the road, later adding a third member to the team to strengthen a new empire we began to build. But as the saying goes, "more money more problems," and that's exactly what came along with our decision.

We traveled back and forth down south to get my hustle on by any means possible. Imagine two young dudes with no license barely able to see over the dashboard and steering wheel pushing these expensive whips. We were so out of control, we were going out of town to hustle in the kitted out whip, system booming and the whole nine. Ridin' dirty with a car full of drugs not even knowing or caring for that matter, that each trip we took we were traveling with a life sentence in the trunk. To us it was simply a way of life. You can get so caught up in the streets that you begin to see nothing wrong with the things you're doing until the day comes when reality jabs the hell out of you square in the face. That day came for me and at the time I had no sense enough to duck when the fun turned serious and the consequences real.

My brother and I were in the South just as much as we were in New Jersey. We were traveling up and down I-95 frequently. The money became plentiful. This was a different type of money and different type of power. We had actually become like our suppliers in The City to the south. In a sense, we had brought New York to them. As long as we were around they never had to worry about running out of product. Usually we took turns making the trip back and forth down south and this particular trip was my brother's turn. For nothing more than my own selfish reasons I convinced him to let me go back to Jersey instead for the re-up. Honestly speaking, I was only eager to get home to see my then girlfriend and show everyone that my brother and I were *"doing our thing out of state."* Something not many, young and old alike from around our way were doing and didn't have heart enough to do back then. We're talking 1988-1989 when it was being reported on the news that many northerners were being murdered in various parts of the south over drug related incidents.

Against his better judgment my brother agreed to let me go this trip. As if he were psychic or probably just knowing me, I remember him saying, *"Yo go straight up and take care of business, then jump on the last bus back down."* That was the plan, but you know in the game nothing goes the way you plan especially at age sixteen.

When I reached Jersey I mixed business with pleasure and that would have grave consequences. This was the first experience I had with being incarcerated for drug trafficking and learning the age difference between being considered an adult or minor when breaking the law. Because I took a detour from the initial agenda I knew I should have followed and really had no business doing what I was doing in the first place I found myself in the midst of a routine bus stop and search in Raleigh North Carolina.

Unbeknownst to me at the time, I had fit the ideal description or rather stereo-type of someone who could possibly be committing a crime to the police who were posted up at the bus terminal. This is what they had to go on. I was a young African-American male traveling alone with a one-way ticket from New York to South Carolina during school hours. A suspicion and hunch, which by the way is against the law according to the Fourth Amendment, is what ultimately lead to my arrest. I was given a $50,000 bail which they wanted $7,500 and a co-signer because I was from out of state.

Thinking back I believe it was meant for me to remain in the Wake county jail for nearly two months as a wake up call, but I just didn't get it. I was still asleep mentally and was still disregarding all the signs that were put before me. If we just follow the signs they will point us in the right direction. How ironic is this. I should have never spent a day in jail, not when my brother was out but things beyond are control were happening which made me feel that I should've been where I was back then. My first bail money was given to my mother by my brother to bail me out, but before she was able to come post it her husband had stolen and did up until this day I don't know what.

The second time my brother and friends came down to post it and was stopped by police because his car fit the description of a KFC that had just been robbed and the money was confiscated. When he finally did post my bail, I decided not to return to court to face the charges since I had given them a fictitious name anyway, not realizing how that too would come back to haunt me. We have a tendency of digging a ditch for ourselves until it becomes so deep that when we fall in it we can't climb out. As stated earlier, I had no respect for the law, I lived life lawlessly.

Eventually, while being on the run from my case in North Carolina I caught a bunch of juvenile charges called secret indictments, which I was being accused and later found guilty of serving controlled dangerous substances to under-cover police officers. In the middle of the night they kicked in me and brother's house door and arrested me.

Fortunately for me, my brother, and his then girlfriend at the time, the warrant was only for me and not to search the house, because had it been, there were enough drugs in it to send all of us away for a nice amount of time. Needless to say, as I sat, fought, and served my time for the juvenile charges, the charges in North Carolina re-surfaced and I had to face the music.

This misfortune cost me nineteen months out of my life in an adult prison at age sixteen. I was transported to North Carolina from New Jersey in a blue Crown Victoria by two officers. I was sentenced to seven years in prison. Could you imagine going to adult prison, not the youth house, at age sixteen. It also cost me to lose the then girlfriend and child she was carrying at the time when she decided to have an abortion.

I can't stress to you enough the severity of the wrong choices and decisions we make. Incarceration puts a drastic strain on relationships and often destroys them. It did it to my mother and our family, it did it to my brother and his, and it did it to me and mine. You would think that my losses would've been enough to make me change my life or even think to back then, but that was far from the case.

The only good thing that came out of this situation was me continuing my education and eventually receiving a diploma before I was released.

During this short period of incarceration I did what I had to do to project an appearance of change, going through the motions as a form of manipulation of the system. Many of us have mastered that art of manipulation as a means of getting what we want, but one thing about deceiving someone or faking them out is, you may be able to fool them but you can not fool yourself. The truth of the matter is I was working on and focusing on becoming a better criminal.

My criminal thinking was in over-drive as I connected with other criminal thinkers in the North Carolina adult facility, gathering new contacts, and counting down the days until I was able to get back to business. Besides, my brother was still out there representing for the both of us. I wasn't ready to change, nor did I feel there was a need to. You have to want to change. You have to consciously, mentally, and verbally say to yourself, **Enough Is Enough,** and at that point in my life I was not ready or prepared to do that. If I had somehow managed to see the wisdom in changing, my brother had made it hard for me to do so anyway.

 I walked right back into the street life the first day I was released. During those nineteen months my brother made sure I wanted or needed for nothing. He took care of me while I was away and when I came home he made sure I wanted or needed for nothing. He provided me with all the hustler accessories; a car, money, jewelry and a crew he put together. Within a week's time I was back knee deep in the game. I got my hustle swagger back and it was as if I had never spent one day in prison.

There's a saying that goes, *"if you fail to plan then you plan to fail."* And that's the best way to describe what took place with me. I had basically failed the first day I was released from prison, like so many brothers and sisters do, because the only plan I had was really no plan at all. My returning to prison was inevitable. This was the first time I had actually experienced that shine I spoke about earlier coming home from prison.

I had gone from 114lbs to 150lbs, and for my height of 5ft 5', at eighteen years old, that was big for me. It seemed like my name was being spilled out of everyone's mouth, male and female. I fell victim hard and fast to the façade and bought in to the hype surrounding it. The fact that my brother had climbed in the game financially and status wise only heightened my new found instant fame and status.

The union between my brother and I was that of a movie. Because my brother was not only my brother, but my best friend, and a male role model for me in my life it made it that ,much more easier for me to resort back and embrace what I was use to doing. Had I come home and discovered my brother had turned over a new leaf I'm sure it would have influenced me in some way to strive for the same, later that would rang true. Only home a few weeks, I allowed my new status, reputation, not to mention my mouth getting me into a situation with the law. Prior to coming home, confrontations between police and hustlers had erupted in my hometown.

Just days before I had come home it had struck my own home. My brother had been the victim of a police assault around the housing projects we grew up in after attempting to elude them. My first day home, when he opened the door to greet me, the first thing I noticed was the scab wound which covered at least thirty percent of his forehead. The sight angered me and I remembered saying, "If I was home it wouldn't have went down like that." I don't profess to be a killer or this great fighter, but when it came to my brother, there was no telling what I would have been capable of.

One uneventful evening while preparing to attend a Super-Bowl party police rolled up around our neighborhood and gave chase to a family member of mine who at the time had a warrant for his arrest but was unsuccessful at apprehending him because he had made it inside the building and closed the door on them. The sight of them triggered something inside of me. They weren't even concerned with me but I was concerned with them.

My brother and my friends discussed amongst themselves how tired they were of what was taking place, I on the other hand voiced my views loud enough for the officers to hear, drawing attention to myself. "As long as they don't touch you (my brother) or none of ya'll (my friends), f-them jokers." The officers wasted no time confronted me, knowing I was referring to them. "My man, get against the gate," one of the officers ordered. The were both African American, which meant nothing to me, especially remembering my first encounter with a black officer. "For what?" I rebelled. That's when he tried to make me comply, ending in a riot amongst what seemed like the entire Plainfield police department and a few of my street colleagues.

That was actually my first official felony as an adult in the state of New Jersey, but it wouldn't be my last. There after, my brother and I found ourselves getting into one physical altercation after the other with authority, something we later on in life we regret. Now some of those same officers acknowledge, applaud, and congratulating us for making that transition by turning our lives around. That's the power of change. For them it was a job, for us it was also a job, now the jobs that we possess do not conflict.

In the short period of time I was on the streets, I managed to father three children, catch numerous cases and become a fugitive of justice. I remember those last days on the streets before I finally caught the case that stuck a fork in me. At the time I was out on three different bails, one $25,000 bail and two $50,000 bails. The crazy thing about it all is that it seemed like every time I went to court to face the charges for the previous case I'd catch a new case on top of it.

One afternoon, after finally agreeing to plead out to a four years sentence with a two years mandatory minimum on the two cases I had pending, I left the court house went back to my town and opened up shop. Needless to say I caught a new charge just hours after signing the papers and awaiting my sentencing date. I'll never forget the words my attorney said to me over the phone that day I called him to inform him of my new case. "Are you insane? Why you keep throwing rocks at these people prisons? You need to switch profession because this one isn't working for you." And he was absolutely right.

My life was in shambles and the streets began to take its toll on me. This was the case that ultimately lead to my going on the run to evade further prosecution and serve time. I committed the crimes, but now here it was I was not ready to do the time. Here it was, my then girlfriend was carrying what would later become my son, my money had depleted due to bails, lawyer fees, and just everyday living expenses, and they wanted me to go off to jail, wasn't happening. So, I packed up all of my belongings, relocated to the south and set back up shop.

It was down there where I truly lost all control of my life. At this point of my life I had acquired the "I don't give an F" attitude. That is when your life becomes so chaotic that you'll do any and everything it takes to survive. My madness was fueled by money and I was making plenty of it. It seemed the more money I made the more risks I would take. Just as a mockery to the system I would travel back through my hometown and old neighborhood on my way to The City to show my peers I was still alive, breathing, and doing what I believed to be big things at the time. I would get phones from friends asking was it true I had come through the area. That would heighten my risk taking, despite the fact that I could have so easily been apprehended being in the wrong place at the wrong time, but by then I was so caught up and high on life that I couldn't see pass the clouds beneath me.

I honestly didn't believe I would caught, something I think every hustler in the game thinks at one point in there illegal career. I remember me and someone on my team from North Carolina were traveling on The New Jersey Turnpike north bound headed to The City when we were stopped by a State Trooper. I was asleep while this dude had been clocked doing over ninety miles per hour. I awake to a flash light shinning in my face, and I'm thinking to myself, "This is it, they got me." If looks could kill, they would have already lowered the drivers casket into the ground and covered him with dirt.

Here it was I had $26,000 in the pockets of my North Face snorkel and this dude is speeding. On top of that, the troopers smelled marijuana pouring out of the car window as if the driver had just moments ago been chewing it like tobacco. In spite of all of that, due to it being the wee hour of the night, the fact that the driver handed over the six personal bags of marijuana he had to one of the troopers, and there shift was soon to be over (from what they said) they only issued a ticket and said we could be on our way once they pat searched us.

I had already chalked the money up as a lost once I was asked to step out of the vehicle. When his hand hit the Goose Down of my jacket he asked, "What's that?" My reply, "My money." I already knew the next question before he'd asked. "How much you got?" "About twenty-six," I answered leaving it at that hoping he'd done the same. But he didn't. "Twenty-six hundred?" I started to say yeah, but at age nineteen, even that seemed to be too much for him. "Grand," I said.

Where he was once paled faced he now became red as Ruldoph's nose. He called over to his partner, "We got us some drug dealers." Instantly my mind began to go into survival mode. I began to tell him how I was a college student and my mother had wired me the money down from Indianapolis so I could purchase a car to get around, and that because I was up north I was coming to buy my car from up there because they much cheaper. It came out so smooth and consistent that I myself believed it, but the trooper didn't.

Still his actions surprised me. "Look it hear, I know you two are going to New York to get you about a kilo or more of the cocaine and try to take it back down south and sale it. I'm not going to take that money even though I should, but what I am going to do is take this license plate number down and send it down this highway so that every trooper from here to North Carolina can be on the look out when you try to go back down with them drugs." I maintained my story but in my mind I'm thinking, "What the hell."

Whether he was capable of doing what he said or not, his threat and the fact that I had been spared from being imprisoned that day was enough to delay me from turning back around and traveling down the highway but it was not enough to stop me from making my intended purchase. I had put myself in life-threatening situations and committed acts that would have put me under the jail had I been caught on numerous occasions and I caused my loved ones to lose plenty of sleep over the life I was living.

My mother would always fret about getting that dreadful phone call or late night knock on the door, telling her I was found dead somewhere. I remember how one out of many of my violent acts had affected one of my younger sisters. During this time, my brother had been incarcerated from charges he had caught prior and after I had come home, so I was now left by myself to "hold it down." I followed the traditional behavior my brother and I were known for of "getting' money." As my wealth grew, so did my enemies.

One particular time an altercation transpired between someone from a past rivalry block over a female. The incident resulted into gun-play after I had previously initiated it by whipping out a 44 snub nosed, threatening to use if I ever ran into them again, and then stupidly letting a few rounds off in the air before I made my get-a-way. Later they came to my block for retaliation. I remember in the midst of the arising altercation my mother's brand-new red Acura Integra coming from under the bridge of the projects.

I am the only reason why my mother would even visit the projects or come down the particular street so I knew she was coming to see me. In my mind I'm thinking, "I got this gun on me and I know I'm about to use it, damn can't let my moms be in the cross fire." Mind you, it's me versus thirteen dudes, one from town, the other twelve out-of-towners, so I'm also thinking, thirteen dudes= thirteen guns (later I found out they only had one amongst them all and only came to fight).

At the time they were questioning a street associate of mine of my whereabouts. They hadn't seen me coming from behind them, but I saw them. It was an advantage that I had. As a means to alert my mother of the potential danger she was about to be faced with I made my way into the middle of street and drew my gun just as she was about to pull over and stop seeing my presence. Judging by her sudden acceleration I knew she had gotten the picture. Not only had she saw me with weapon in hand, those who were looking for me had saw me as well. "There he go right there," the kid from my town called out. Whatever was said after that was cut short as the thunder of my long nosed 357 roared in their direction. "BOOM, BOOM, BOOM," they rang out in succession. As the fourth shot followed suit someone ran into and grabbed hold of me, causing the fifth shot to travel into the window of a friend of mines.

When I looked it was my little sister. She was crying and screaming, "No don't kill my brother." Even though shot were not being returned, the impact the incident had on my sister that day was so traumatizing for her and emotional for me to the point that she did not and will not remember that day until she reads it in this book and I never spoke about it up until now.

I shared this piece of my chaotic life style I once lived as an eye-opener of how our loved ones are affected by our behavior. That day, I didn't kill anyone, but I could have easily had. There were times when I was not the one behind the gun but on the other side of the barrel. I'd been shot twice over materialistic items and mere words. Can you imagine how my loved ones felt to receive that phone call saying, "Your son or daughter etc has been shot and is in the hospital."

I remember one year, I had so much beef and was shooting so much that when I finally was arrested my older sister wrote me a letter and it opened it with, "Hey bro, hope all is well with you despite where you are. To be truthful, don't take this wrong way, but I'm glad you are where you are, now me, mommy, and our little sister (sister's name best left out) came sleep better at night." I couldn't believe what I had read, but I understood. How could someone have a good night's rest knowing that those who they loved lives or freedom could be taken away from them any second of the day due to the life styles they lived. When I was finally apprehended my reckless lifestyle finally caught up to me.

I received a lengthy prison sentence by the state and then afterwards a lengthy federal prison sentence to drive the point home because I had yet to learn a lesson, the right one anyway. When it was all said and done, in total, I gave the system over twelve years of my thirty-four years of living.

Prison Life

When I entered into the state prison it was like a madhouse. It was thee most educational, degrading, disrespectful time I've ever had to endure in my life. I literally felt like a caged animal, only eventually after getting caught up in the prison politics, I became just that. I was given a total of eighteen months in lock-up and only allowed to have visitation with loved ones from behind a plexi-glass partition because of my involvement with selling drugs in prison.

While in solitary confinement an elderly inmate who had served time with my father and uncle in the seventy's and eighty's was the tier's porter. Judging by his appearance and the look in his eyes, I could tell he had lived a rough and hard life, one far more extensive then my own, but nonetheless similar. His face was filled with old scars and wounds, each one I'm sure that had a story of its own. His forearms were bloated, complimentary of the healed up track marks scattered through-out them. His eyes were that of black marbles, and he possessed a salt and pepper beard that hung down to his chest. As he cleaned the tier and passed the telephone from cell to cell each day he'd often interrupt my reading time to hold a conversation with me.

I always spoke highly of my father and uncle and tell war stories of their past prison times in various facilities. He told me things about my father that I never knew but found myself comparing to myself, and thinking, "Here it is I'm doing the same thing my pops was doing decades ago in similar facilities.

I would wonder why the elder took a liking to me and spent his free time out of his cell talking to me until one day he revealed his intentions. This particular day he asked me did I believe in God. I told him how my mother was a minister and how I had grown up in the church. I asked me what I knew about Muslims and Islam. I was somewhat knowledgeable but no where near the extent of what he was saying. I don't know why I attentively listened as he spoke about Allah because at the time I was un-interested in religion, but what rang out to me the most as he spoke is how he kept saying, "Allah saved my life."

Before it was time for the elder to lock back in to his cell he asked the officer could he give me a book. He then slid the book under my door way and said, "I always see you reading, read this." The book was titled "Tauhid (The Oneness Of God)". Out of the respect I had for the elder I began to read it. That evening I stayed up all night until I finished the book from cover to cover, then I started it again the next day. It was through that book that God touched my heart and caused me to embraced Islam in prison while down Trenton State prison.

Islam enabled me to find peace of mind and learn what it consisted of to be a man. In state prison in the beginning it was a constant struggle for me to maintain that peace of mind because I was so rebellious and reckless with my behavior. Every man/woman is afforded the same opportunity in prison.

There are many things made available to you for the embitterment or the destruction of your life for when you return back to society. Slowly but surely during that time I was trying to change. I had gotten caught up and sucked into the negativity that one can succumb to in prison and was now trying to find a way out. Nevertheless, I had worked on changing for the six years when I was in the state, but deep down inside I knew I hadn't changed enough. When I entered the federal prison system, the reality of the further changes I needed to make began to set in.

My first family visit in Federal prison, minus any partitions, came when my mother flew in from Indianapolis to see me for my birthday. Prior to this visit, my mother had visited me in prison before but now that there was no plexiglass partition to separate us this visit was the most emotional visit the two of us had ever had.

I'll never forget the look in my mother's eyes. For a minute she just stared at me and I remember asking her what was wrong. *"I cannot do this any more son this is it",* she said as tears began to spill out her eyes, painting her face as they cascaded down her cheeks. In this very emotional moment I realized just how much pain I was causing my mother; the very woman who brought me into this world. I felt ashamed. Ashamed I had hurt my mother in some of the same ways my father had hurt her. It was hard for me to reach out and console my mother knowing that I too had become the source of her pain.

Because of the guilt I felt, it was hard for me to reach out to my mother for the first few months when I was transferred to federal prison. In many ways the plexi-glass partition that separated us in the state visitation room served as a buffer zone between me, her, and the pain I caused her. Now seeing my mother with nothing standing between us was painful. My reckless lifestyle, rash decisions and lust for the streets had caused my mother so much hurt and I didn't know how to tell her how truly sorry I was. I knew one day I would show her though.

My mother had always been there for me unconditionally and had it not been for a letter she had written me, I don't think I would've known how to reach out to her while I remained in prison after returning back. I remember feeling so ashamed and just feeling that I had let her down. As I sat in my room and began to read the letter my mother had written, the opening lines stood out to me as if I was reading them with 3-D glasses on. Her first words opened a spigot of tears to the point of almost making the letter unreadable. These were the words that had broken me down like a double barreled shotgun.

"Dear son, I want you to know that no matter what, I will always be proud to have you as my child and I will always love you."

No matter how far I had fallen in life my mother had always been there to pick me up. When I forgot who I was and what I was capable of, she was always there to remind me that I could do bigger and better things. I had taken my mother through so much and with her soothing words she was able to ease the guilt that I had been carrying with me all these years, in a way only a mother could do.

My Transitional Process

It was during this period of my life I was in the process of making major transitions for the better. You see, everyone has a limitation in life and I believe I had finally reached mine. I began to really evaluate my life. I started by weighing the pros and the cons of my choices, my actions and my thinking. And at the end of my tally I came to the conclusion that, in spite of what I thought was living the good life when I was hustlin' in the streets, when it was all said and done none of it had been worth it. The materialistic creature comforts that I had accumulated and enjoyed for a short period of time wasn't worth sacrificing my freedom, nor the relationship with my mother and all the other people who cared for me for all those years. If I tallied up all the money I made versus all the years I spent incarcerated, someone with a regular minimum wage job would have made money then I had without visiting any prison.

I knew then that I needed a change from within and the only way I could do that was, by making the decision to do so. I sought guidance in my religious belief and began participating in some of the programs available to me inside the institution. Every man/ woman is afforded the same opportunities in prison, the choices are simply yours. Once I was able to break out of the stereo-typical prison politics such as hometown and territorial confrontations with other inmates, drug selling, and many other contrabands etc. not permissible in the facility, I was able to clear my mind and free it of the imprisonment I had placed it in. It was during that time that one of those programs that a teacher helped me discover my writing. This teacher had advised me to keep a journal and use it as an outlet whenever I felt stressed, discouraged or even encouraged.

Initially, I wasn't feeling this but out of respect for her I calmly accepted the notebook and promised to utilize it. Prison life being what it is, even after all of the self-reconstruction I had been doing, I still managed to return to solitary confinement for a frivolous confrontation that turned into something physical. A few days later the teacher had come to see me in lockup. I was somewhat embarrassed to tell her what had happened knowing how she had held me in such high regard. She treated me not as an inmate but as a human being.

After I explained what happened I still remember what she said in response, *"sometimes things happen and we can't let them get in the way of what we have to do in life. Why don't you take your journal and use it to write about your life and maybe you'll figure out where you keep going wrong."*

Who would've thought those words would have such a major impact on my life and play such a decisive role in securing my future. As suggested, I began to utilize the journal book. Beginning with my earliest recollections as a child of a dysfunctional family I examined the behavior of my parents, particularly my father.

What started out as a therapeutic phase for me blossomed into a four plus page manuscript about me and my brother's life. And even though this was not the material that would eventually land me a two book publishing contract it was the material that motivated me to continue my writing and strive for a career in the literary field. Since discovering what I believe to be one of my many hidden talents, writing had become the basis of my life and a form of discipline for me. Rather than participate in some of the unhealthy or stagnant activities one will find in prison I chose to commit myself to perfecting my craft. The way I see it, when I was out in the streets hustling I had dedicated all of my time and energy into doing that. I figured the same energy I had used then for something negative could be channeled into something positive now.

An old head had told me once that, *"there is a difference between a drug dealer and a hustler."* He'd say, *"they are not one of the same."* The old head explained it like this, *"the drug dealer can only sell drugs. The hustler can sell anything."* Since I've been writing I have proven to myself and to those who matter to me most that I am not a mere drug dealer, but a natural born Hustler. I have grown in all aspects, not only as a writer, but as a man, a father and son, brother and friend.

In 2004, while in federal prison I was fortunate to land a publishing deal. By that time I had been writing for three years. As fate would have it, after years of determination and persistency, when I was transferred to the east side of Fort Dix federal institution an inmate who was not only an avid reader but had ties to the African American lit world read my manuscript he had heard so much about (Down In The Dirty) and referred me to an independent publishing house by the name of Flowers In Bloom Publishing.

It was through Nancey Flowers CEO of FIBP that the world was introduced to author J.M. Benjamin. Down In The Dirty was released and available in all stores four months before my release, shortly thereafter I made my feature debut in an anthology published by Melodrama Publishing titled Menace II Society. At the time I was released from federal prison and turned over to New Jersey Department of Corrections to finish out a state prison term. I remember receiving a copy of both the anthology and Down In The Dirty sitting in my single six by nine cell. I was speechless. A wide grin appeared on my face as I sat on the bed saying, "This shit is real." As I cracked Down In The Dirty open and began to read tears begin to drip from my eyes. Not because the story was so emotional for me to read but because I was responsible for the pages in which I was reading. These pages represented more then just a good read for me. They represented my journey of change and how far I had come. They represented my life. Most of all, they represented each and every last one that comes from and has gone through what I had.

In 2006, Mid State Correction Facility granted me community release, ultimately sending me to The Talbot Hall assessment center/C.E.C program. It was there at Talbot Hall where my life as I knew it was changed forever and I discovered new things about myself and came in contact with new people. While a resident at Talbot Hall, the benefits of all of my hard work with my writing had finally paid off.

My freshman novel Down In The Dirty was released and swept the urban literature genre by storm, opening doors for me and paving a way in society that I had never thought possible. In addition, Talbot Hall became a stepping stone, a polisher, and positive re-enforcement system for me, particularly when I was introduced to The Alumni Organization. I remember attending my first Alumni meeting at Talbot Hall, how the heart felt stories were so impacting upon.

I remember wondering would I be able to get up in front of a room full of people and share my story. Would I be able to get out there and live day by day, one step at a time, and not look back? Would I give the proper answers and best answers when I return back out there and face the biggest test of my life? After attending my first meeting, I knew The Alumni was something that would be for the em-betterment of my self, so I went and joined. It wasn't until I joined and became the Alumni clerk assistant while still a resident at Talbot Hall that I fully realized that I not only joined an organization but gained a new family, family that has proved to be there genuinely for me through thick and thin.

Everyone, whether ex-offender or has never gone to prison, needs a support system, and the Alumni is a part of mine. The Alumni has supported me in my recovery of criminality addiction, morally, mentally, spiritually, emotionally, etc. I am now a 2x Award Winning and Essence Best Selling author, a publisher, motivational speaker, a book store owner, and a distributor. In all that I have accomplished, The Alumni has contributed in some form or fashion to my continuing success. The Alumni is a part of me and I am a part them.

Through Alumni, I am able to return back to male/ female facilities and share my success story and testimony in hopes that I may encourage, inspire, or motivate another or others. For me, prison was a necessary journey and stepping stone in order for me to get my life back on the right track. Prison is what you make of it. Regardless to its conditions and what you're subjected to, Our Higher Power whether it be God or something greater then one's self, has instilled in us all 'free will' and you have a choice to make the necessary changes in your life. So it is up to you to make the best out of what you feel or believe to be the worse.

I made up my mind that once released I would all not return. While incarcerated I worked on changing myself from my attitude all the way down to the way I view things, but most importantly I changed my game plan upon my release. Then when I was released I began to incorporate all that I had learned and been taught out here in the free world. Since life after incarceration I was acknowledged by the C.E.C. program and my Alumni family for my beating the odds attitude. I in return acknowledge them as well for being a creditor to my attitude.

Alumni Spotlight: **It's Never too Late to Change**
October 2007

"It's never too late to change your game plan and make better choices and decisions," according to J. M. Benjamin, a reformed drug dealer, Talbot Hall alumnus, motivational speaker, and award winning author in the growing genre of urban fiction.

Benjamin's decision to change his own game plan and pursue a path other than crime did not happen over night. Instead, his decision mirrored one of Community Education Center's motivational slogans that says, "Change is a Process, Not an Event," and Benjamin admits he encountered many detours along his path before being inspired to begin to change his thinking prior and while participating in CEC's Talbot Hall program in Kearny, New Jersey.

Like the central character in his second novel, <u>My Manz And 'Em,</u> Benjamin grew up in the housing projects in Plainfield, New Jersey and quickly learned to live life on the streets as a hustler. With his father in prison and his mother somewhat absent due to her heavy work schedule, Benjamin had the misfortune of being influenced by his surroundings, including family members who were drug addicts and dealers. Following in their footsteps, Benjamin teamed up with neighborhood friends and began to climb the criminal ladder, selling drugs at the tender age of 12.

By 13, Benjamin had already gone through New Jersey's juvenile correctional facility multiple times, a badge of honor he says he wore with pride. Benjamin explains that when you grow up on the streets, "Doing time earns you instant status in the hood among peers." This newfound respect further fueled what Benjamin describes as his addiction to criminal behavior. However, years later, as a young adult and seasoned veteran in the streets, Benjamin found himself back behind bars, where he served more than twelve years of his life between the state and federal system.

While serving time in a federal prison, Benjamin was drawn to the adventure and antics of urban fiction and became an avid reader. He quickly noticed a disconnection between the books he read and the reality of street life. Whereas the books glamorized gangs and criminal quests, they did not portray prison life and the inevitable ramifications of riding the criminal wave in the depths or light he felt needed to be. As Benjamin would later learn at Talbot Hall, inevitably he would have to accept responsibility for his choices in life.

In addition to reading in prison, Benjamin had begun writing about his childhood and experiences after a counselor gave him a journal and encouraged him to do so. "Writing was therapeutic," says Benjamin, and before he knew it he ended up with a 400-page manuscript about him and his brother's dangerous life style at young ages, then challenged his self to write another, which turned into his first novel, <u>Down In The Dirty</u>. The book was released in 2006 while Benjamin was still serving time. Shortly thereafter, Benjamin found himself at Talbot Hall.

Although proud of his success as an author, Benjamin credits his experience at Talbot Hall with preparing him for "The biggest test of my life—coming home." Inspired by CEC's Alumni Director, Keith Hooper, Benjamin says it was while he was at Talbot hall that he was even more motivated to change and turn his life around then he had ever been.

"Talbot hall was the best thing that could have happened to me before my release," says Benjamin. "Talbot instilled in me the importance of being mindful of the decisions and choices I make." The program also "Armed me with the tools and ammunition I needed to allow me to remain at home," Benjamin explains, commenting that since his release from Talbot Hall in May of 2006, he has had a new outlook on life.

Rather than returning to his career as a criminal, Benjamin says, "I was ready to climb a new ladder and take a better path." He made the conscious choice to focus on living right, helping others, and giving back to society. This time, "I felt I had a positive product to market," he adds, referring to his books. In sharp contrast with many of the novels he has read in prison, Benjamin's writing depicts the authenticity of street life and the consequences of crime. "I wanted to send a provocative message and show that the bad guy never gets away," he said. "Because I never got away." Upon his release, Benjamin won an award for his freshman novel at The African American Literary Awards in 2006 for Best Street Fiction Of The Year.

According to Benjamin, one reason CEC's programs work is because they teach individuals to recognize and accept their addictions and to learn how to identify trigger points as a mechanism for preventing relapse. Benjamin also credits CEC's Alumni Association for providing him with continued support and encouragement after his release.

"The Alumni organization has been more than a support group; it has been a family to me, even to this day," notes Benjamin. "It helped give me the confidence to pursue my dreams," adds Benjamin, who in addition to starting his own publishing company also recently opened a bookstore in downtown Plainfield with the hopes of providing a literary hub for local urban youth to gather. Benjamin's has a third novel titled Ride Or Die Chick scheduled to be released November 2007. "I'm just trying to be consistent, that's really what it's about, consistency," he says.

Today, thanks largely to the support of other CEC alumni and his commitment to remaining crime free, Benjamin uses his talent to write, and his experiences and the knowledge he learned from Talbot hall to speak at high school and college forums, probation and religious programs for the youth, and institutions for incarcerated men and women. Through written and spoken words, Benjamin strives to captivate an audience to convey positive messages with the hopes of inspiring others. Citing one of CEC's motivational slogans, Benjamin adds, "Change is Possible."

"Writing and Islam Saved My Life."

Saturday, March 31st, 2007   Posted by devil advocate in Uncategorized

These words resonated through my soul as "Best New Street Author of the Year -2006," at the African American Literary Awards J. M. Benjamin sincerely recited his gratitude for being incarcerated.

That's right, gratitude! *"Didn't think writing would help me stay off the streets and talk about what's important to me."* The author of (short story) "Keeping it Gangsta," (novels) <u>Down in the Dirty</u>, and <u>My Manz and 'Em</u> visited Paterson on Saturday, March 24, 2007 at NU Expression art gallery.

His street beginning has been a vehicle for his positive destiny. This Plainfield, NJ native uses his knowledge and experience today to write books and convey positive messages through urban lingo in his racy, but real-life settings with the hopes of captivating an audience that will utilize his themes as proactive and preventive measures for prison. *"I am blessed and would like to continue giving back to my community."* Since the age of 12, J. M. Benjamin has had the misfortune of experiencing the *game*, but somewhere has managed to vehemently realize that it's not too late to change. As a result, he is a motivational speaker – speaking at high school and college forums regarding his books and *how to change the game*. Also, he is the founder and co-owner of Real Edutainment Publishing which published his sophomore novel <u>My Manz and 'Em</u> released February 2007. J.M Benjamin has been featured on the

Wendy Williams Experience as the book of the month in July 2006, and is currently nominated for two awards, by the Chicago Black Authors and Books Awards in May 2007. When asked how it feels to be an author and sell a story as a product instead of something else he stated, "*I don't consider myself an author, but a storyteller. I was always a great speaker, but the way I tell my story is what has allowed me this opportunity.*" And obviously, he tells it well. Lastly, J. M. was recently promoted on the Michael Baisden show highlighting his motivational engagements, and book signings that could be found on AllAboutJMBenjamin.com.

J.M. Benjamin would like to make urban lit genre *authentic* by demonstrating his keen sense of the street and transferring it onto paper; sending provocative messages, and depicting a culture that is frequently overlooked in literature. The *Game* continues…

On July 3, 2006, I was released from custody. I remember waking that morning and thinking, "This is it, the closing of an old chapter and the opening of a new beginning." I was so focused that nothing or no one could break my spirits or still my joy, not even when I was told they're was a delay in my release due to some paper work issues. Had I not prepared myself for any and everything I could have easily become frustrated or acted out emotionally to further delay the closing of that chapter of my life. In prison I had learned to have patience and to use my intellect over my emotions. A lot of times, my temper combined with my mouth got me in situations I could have so easily avoided, making my stay in prison a little longer then it should have been and making my time that much harder to serve. Through-out my process of change and making that transition I learned to identify my triggers. For me, my triggers were how I perceived things and the way I handled them once I formed a perception. This time I recognized this was my first test, sort of like a pop quiz before the final exam, and I was ready. I had long ago studied and prepared for any and all tests that would come my way. I had already made up my mind and told myself that failure was not an option. Those of you who come from what I do have to tell yourselves that and then listen to your own words because sometimes it's not embraced properly or well coming from someone else, especially if you're the type that feels no one can tell you what's best for YOU. Once I began to believe I knew better I began to do better. As I patiently waited on one side of the facility my family await on the opposite side. My mother had driven from Illinois to Indianapolis to pick my sisters and nephews up then drove hundreds of miles to New Jersey to be there for my release. The night prior, my mother and I were having a conversation and I could hear in her tone how tired she was. Wanting to be considerate of the fact, I insisted she'd come after I was released and her response melted my heart like fried ice cream in mid July. "No, I'm okay, I told you along time ago the day they released you I would be there waiting. This is my day and I'm not going to miss it." And she was right this was not only my day, but hers as well. She was the one who had done day for day- year in year out with me, so how could I deny my mother her release date of all the pain, stress, lack of rest, wasted money, etc because of me? That last phone conversation with my mother as an inmate was just more confirmation of what I needed to do, not only as a son, but a father, brother, and man. When I finally stepped out of the facility my mother/support system was there for me with opened arms. It had been a long time since I had seen her face lit up the way it had been that day. I waked into her embrace and wrapped my arms around her tightly. It was an emotional scene for the both of us. The reality instantly kicked in that I was a free man. I took a deep breath and took in the freshness of air then released my mother from the bear hug I had her wrapped in. It felt good to be home. As I made my way over to the passenger side I saw caught my mother wiping her eye from under her glasses. I knew it felt good for her to have me home too.

Upon my release reality began to set in. For a split second my biggest fear over came me. "Would something from my past come back to haunt me?" You see, we have to realize that just because we've changed doesn't mean everything and everyone else has. We also have to realize that just because we've changed for the better, still, we are not exempt from being targeted or subjected to what once landed us behind those prison walls. We as ex-offenders must work that much harder to remain out of the lions den

On **July 4, 2006**, my second day home that fear was replaced. During the Fourth Of July Parade, I due to no African American book store being in my hometown, I held a book signing out front of my long time friend Butch Webb's barbershop and was well embraced by my peers. Brother's I had once went to war against in these very same streets came out to support and women who I once may have treated wrongly or disrespectfully when I lived a different type of life style came out to support me. It was that day that I experienced the power of change. What I partook in and where I came from did not define who I was that day. That day and days and years there after I was not a drug dealer, a gangsta, a thug, etc. I was J.M. Benjamin the author and now I am J.M. Benjamin the publisher, book store owner, distributor, and motivational speaker. Because I believed in myself and wanted better for myself, I literally went from the trials and tribulations during incarceration and overcoming them to incorporation after I was released, becoming a productive citizen in society. This is my story…This is my reality…It can be yours too!

City author brings streets to bookstores
Plainfield store features urban fiction titles.
By BERNICE PAGLIA
CORRESPONDENT

PLAINFIELD -- Selling drugs landed him in prison. Now, J.M. Benjamin is selling his urban fiction novels to eager customers at book events nationwide. But in his Queen City hometown, the place where he wanted most to hold book signings, there was no bookstore.

The former-inmate-turned-author decided to do something about it, so he has launched a book outlet featuring the wildly popular urban fiction genre, along with other titles and children's books, inside Music N Motion at 204 East Front St. Next month, residents need only to go downtown to get a signed copy of his third novel, "Ride or Die Chick."

It was barely a month ago that Benjamin approached Don Benito, owner of Music N Motion, to ask if he could set up a display table in front of the store. Benito welcomed him inside, and Benjamin's first small selection has since more than tripled.

"I have brought a new element to downtown Plainfield," Benjamin said.

Benjamin said buyers, mostly young people who did not read much before, are buying 80 to 100 books a week.

The store previously sold mainly CDs, DVDs and Leonard Benjamin's "Ghettofficial Designs" custom T-shirts. Benito's wife, Kimberly, said all three of her daughters -- Shayna, 15; Christina, 21; and Keyna, 22 -- have taken up reading since Benjamin brought his books to the store. None were readers before, she said.

Kimberly Benito said urban fiction lets young people understand what's out on the streets.

"You have to educate children and make them aware of what's going on," she said.

Plainfield librarian Lonnie Johnson agreed that the genre has exploded.

"They are reading it, and they are reading it furiously," he said.

Some have compared the fervor of young adults for urban fiction with that of grade school children for Harry Potter.

The content of urban fiction -- drugs, sex, violence, street language -- is controversial to many, but Johnson said, "Reading is a skill that once you've acquired, you can move on to other things."

Benjamin's strategy since publication of his first award-winning book, "Down in the Dirty," has been to meet potential readers where they can be found, in urban barbershops, gathering places and neighborhoods. Some of his travels are along the same highways and streets where he used to ply his drug trade. Benjamin said the drive that would send him out in any weather to sell drugs now has been transferred to "something positive."

On the first day he began the book outlet, he went from the city's East End to the West End, distributing fliers. He also did an e-mail blitz to alert his fans.

Benjamin's allegiance to his hometown also is reflected in his story of betrayal, "My Manz and 'Em," which features a cover photo of the public housing project where he once lived. The book is peppered with references to real Plainfield and Central Jersey businesses and alludes to city turf wars. But it does not glorify the life of its characters.

"You'll never purchase a J.M. Benjamin book where the bad guy gets away," he said. "I didn't get away, so my characters don't get away."

Benjamin expects his newfound ties to urban fiction writers will bring many of the authors to the city for book signings in the future. "I know them personally," he said.

"Gettin' Money Off the Books" J.M Benjamin: How He Became Successful by Switching Up His Product
by Shakila Singleton

J.M. Benjamin is an author from Plainfield, NJ that changed his life around by trading in the drug game for a pen and a pad. In a short period of time, he has gone from a convicted felon to a successful author. He is set to release his third novel, *Ride or Die Chick,* through Flowers in the Bloom Publishing on December 7, 2007. J.M. Benjamin's success began with his debut novel *Down in the Dirty* which won an award for best street novel in the African American Literary awards in September of 2006 and book of the year at the Infini 1st Literary Awards on May 17, 2007.

Though *Down in the Dirty* continued to sell out in stores, JM Benjamin released his sophomore novel *My Manz and Em* on February 14, 2007 through Real Edutainment Publishing. The success of *My Manz and Em* proves that the success of the first novel was not a fluke. He also contributed to Nikki Turner's *Christmas in the Hood (Street Chronicles)* which was released this fall. His third novel drops in December J.M. Benjamin is making noise and he's definitely trying to show us he's in the building. His books are available at many major stores including Target, Borders, Waldens, Barnes & Noble, and Amazon.com. In addition, through his publishing company, his books can also be shipped to prisons. *SWeT Magazine* had the opportunity to meet up with this hard working author on a few occasions, one of those meetings being at a local New Jersey gym, getting his workout on.

SWeT: Can you briefly tell the readers about the plot for My Manz and Em?

JM: My manz and em is a popular saying amongst African Americans in particular but more so in the streets. So when you use it, it's like a term of endearment or to express how you feel about a certain individual. But what *My Manz in Em* is about is the reality of that statement when you are in the game, when you're in the street. When you're in the streets your manz and them are not really your manz and them. So that's what this story's about. It's about when you get knocked off and go to prison. You know, sometimes your manz and em are the cause of that but then, when you go to jail, your manz and them don't send you money, don't except collect calls, don't send you pictures, don't come visit you, don't check up on ya family, try to push up on ya lady, so on and so forth. But, those are "your manz and them." But [in] this particular story, the brother goes down for something regarding his manz and em. So, when he's coming home, he already told himself that he's not dealing with his manz and em anymore. This story's about a dude who just wants to come home and find his place in society, in the workforce with a relationship but, it's hard for him. Why? Because 1) He has limited and minimal job and educational skills and training 2) He's an ex offender 3) He's an African American male and 4) He practices a belief, Islam, that is frowned upon and shunned by many in society.

All of these things he has against him but yet and still, he tries to find balance in the world. So when he comes home, he tries to be a good son, a good man. Then, he meets a companion, a strong black woman who is very independent. She's from the hood but the hood doesn't define her. She has a career, her own money, her own car, her own house, and she doesn't want anything in regards [to] a man other than companionship. I showed how a strong black woman holds down a man throughout his struggle.

SWeT: And that's not the typical image of woman portrayed in street literature. Why did you choose to do otherwise?

JM: (with a charming smile) I write for the ladies so I depicted a female in my story that's outside the norm, outside the box of the women portrayed in street lit books. Normally they take the role of gold diggers, high maintenance [women], chicken heads, hood rats, so on and so forth. So, to show the ladies that there are brothers that do understand and do acknowledge the parts that they play in those type of situations, [I created this character]. And you don't have to go to prison to have a strong woman to hold you down or be by your side. I'm just saying, I write street lit so I wanted to change the perception that they have of my sistas…So even though this brother comes home focused, still he runs into his manz and em and that sets the tone of the story.

At this point we take a break so he can do another set. J.M. walks away to get a heavier set of weights.

SWeT: What impact do you think the streets of Plainfield had on your life, your books?

JM: Actually, because of the environment I grew up in, I grew up in a low [income housing], poverty stricken environment, dysfunctional home, single parent, you know. So like all of that affected me as a kid because when you're a child you're like a sponge. You absorb everything that you come in contact with and you're trying to find your place and your position for when you go into adulthood. So like for me, all I [saw] was drugs, violence, and abuse and so on and so forth, for the most part. I'm not saying my entire life that's all I knew but, for the majority, that's what I was exposed to, having aunts and uncles who used drugs or sold drugs or committed crimes, just living a criminal lifestyle. The only relationship I had with my father as a kid was through prison. I seen my mom struggle, work, and go to school, crying so on and so forth. All of that impacted me. As a child you don't understand the dynamics and depths of what you see but, you know that something is not right. Then, when you see something so much, you begin to believe that *it is right.*

SWeT: And you got your book deal for *Down in the Dirty* while you were still incarcerated, right?

JM: Definitely. I was in federal prison when I started writing.

SWeT: So, you started writing in prison?

JM: Um hm. It's funny because someone bought it to my attention recently, a childhood friend of mine. I used to write poems when I was hustling, when I was in the streets, before prison. So, writing was in me. I just didn't have the right resources or the role models to point me in that direction. If I had to say I had a talent back then, I didn't have someone to nourish and guide me to pursue that. When I went to prison I continued to write poems. It was a side hustle. Writing poems for brothers' ladies, for special occasions, that was a little side gig of mine.

SWeT: How long were you incarcerated?

JM: Between the state and the feds I did 12 1/2 years.

SWeT: What did you go for?

JM: Drug trafficking, racketeering, transporting, conspiracy, a variety of drug charges.

SWeT: A lot of people go away for that long or they may do 5 or 10 years and come home to do what they were doing even harder than before they went in. What made you come home and get on this straight path? What made you make the decision not to go down that road again?

JM: It was a multitude of things. Actually, what happened was when I first I went to prison, I was in the state and I had no intention on changing anything. That's what it really boils down to. The key word in everything is change. I was content with how things [were] going with me. When I got in the game, I felt that the ends justified the means. I'm getting all of this paper. I got a name. I don't want for nothing. Of course jail comes with this. So, I'ma go to jail, get my weight up, get my mind right, and I'ma perfect a plan and come home and go harder. That was my mind frame when I went in. So, when I went, I [saw] that prison was no different than the streets really. I jumped right into it headfirst. So I was hustlin' in jail. Without going into depths, I [saw] a side that many can't talk about in the system from the corruption in which those who work there. Those who take an oath to govern and oversee us [were] worse than us. See what I'm saying. I caught a case in prison, a drug case. Someone set me up. I went to lock up. That really did it cause I lost everything. I was in a situation where I was on the verge of getting engaged. So when I caught a case in jail, because of my name and who I was in my town, I couldn't lie. I couldn't hide what took place. So my lady at the time, when I called, I tried to lie and say that I was locked up for fighting but she knew I caught a charge. So her thing was if you can't stop selling drugs in jail, then how are you gonna come home and stop selling drugs? Which was true. So, because of that, it put a strain on the relationship with my son. Everything, just bad things, was happening. I was like, damn, I know that this isn't my purpose in life. I began to do some soul searching. At the time I had just embraced Islam. I was Muslim but I wasn't ready to submit wholeheartedly back then because my mind was still distorted. I was in lock up for 1 ½ years. All I did was read. I began to get into my belief. That's when I realized that I really wasn't a man [in the past]. That's what Islam teaches you, how to be a man or a woman. It gives you the blueprint on how to live your life in manhood or womanhood. When I made that transition, I began to see everything crystal clear. I decided man, I don't wanna do it no more. I want to go home. I don't want to hustle in jail. I don't want to hustle in the streets. My mom was living in

Indianapolis at the time. I didn't have a female that was holding me down. I didn't have someone who was visiting me regularly. My mom would fly in every month from Indianapolis to visit me. My moms sent me food packages. My moms cried constantly on visits and *all of that* played a part My mom would pick my kids up and bring my kids to see me and my moms said to me "I can't do this no more. What's good?" It didn't push me to writing it just pushed me to change. I had already made a transition before writing.

SWeT: What year was this?

JM: This was 2001. I started writing. Writing changed my life because it was therapeutic for me. It allowed me to see who I really was, and I didn't like what I saw. For others incarcerated, it may be sports, it may be working out, it may be the law library, something but, brothers do their time differently. How you do your time dictates how things will be when you return back to the real world, bottom line. There's a book that a brother named Randy Kearse wrote called *Changing Your Game Plan*. It's about success after incarceration and I contributed my life story to it. Basically, it's saying your life is not over just because you went to prison. Use your time wisely. Find something constructive. Hone in on it. Perfect it. Come home and incorporate it. And like me and this brother Randy, we met in prison. He heard I had a publishing deal. It was circulating through the federal prison that I had a deal, and he wanted to get into writing but didn't know how. So, he came to me and we befriended each other. We used to walk the yard like everyday and I used to tell him like (Smiling and looking up as if totally reminiscing) 'Yo, when I get home they gonna hear me. They gonna hear about me on the radio. They gonna read about me in magazines. They gonna see me in magazines. They gonna see me at the awards and everything' I used to always say that.

SWeT: (laughs) And you made it happen.

JM: And he said 'Man, when you go, just take me with you.' And that's what I do. He and I are motivational speakers. We do speaking engagements together. We do book signings together. So, that right there within itself, we changed the gravity of the laws. We came home and did something other than what they expected. Like generally, when two dudes meet in jail, we're like, Yo, where you from? I'm from here. Then, when we get out, we like, Yo, this move for that much out my way. A yo, we gonna get some paper. But it's an illegal aspect. Me and this brother came home and did something positive. This is my only gig. This is the only job I've eve had in my life. I've never had a 9 to 5.

SWeT: And that's perfect because that's exactly what the magazine is trying to do. We're trying to show people that they can come home and get on some legal shit.

JM: A legal hustle.

SWeT: Exactly.

JM: It's about changing the game plan and switching up your product.

SWeT: Exactly.

JM: People move white Ts, DVDs, oils, incense. **Drugs is like my billion infinity option, meaning it's never gonna be an option for me again.** Now that I know it's something better, I can hustle something better and I'm good at it.

SWeT: And you don't have to look over your back.

JM: Definitely.

SWeT: What type of advice would you give for those that are currently incarcerated and ready to come home or just still bidding?

JM: The change starts from within. You can self prep all you want in prison on the surface you can make it look good whether it's in a sport or religion, but the change starts from within. You can fake any and everybody out on the outside but you can't fake yourself out. If you don't like who you are looking at in the mirror, then change the man in the mirror. Bottom line. It's doable. I'm like a poster child for change right now. It's doable, with dedication, determination, persistence and just staying focused, it's doable. I used to say that the streets was all I knew, the drug game was all I knew. I just used that as a justification, a crutch to keep doing wrong. That's not all we know. That's just what we limit ourselves to. So I'm closing on that. Don't come home and limit yourself.

(We break while he does another set)

SWeT: You said you do speaking engagements and things of that nature, right? Where do you do them?

JM: So far I've spoken at high schools, junior high schools, halfway houses, book clubs, colleges, all in various states. I've spoken in CT, NY, NJ, MD...

SWeT: Now let's go to the novels released this year, *My Manz and Em* and *Ride or Die Chick*. They're published through Real Edutainment publishing. What is Real Edutainment Publishing?

JM: My publishing company is Real Edutainment Publishing and what that provided for is that I just wanted to put out reality stories that are educational and entertaining at the same time and that's what I do. I educate and entertain at the same time…You know what I also wanted the readers to know in regards to Real Edutainment Publishing. How it came about was, there's no African American bookstores in my hometown of Plainfield. I wanted to open up a bookstore, not only for my town, but for my children to have somewhere to grow up in, to see the business side of the world, somewhere to hang out, see something positive and they can pick up a book. They say that our youth, our people, don't read as much as they should. They used to have all types of sayings like if you want to hide something from a black, put it in a book. I wanted them to know that everything they needed to know was in a book. I told a childhood friend of mine, Kevin R. White that I wanted to open this bookstore and I was looking for investors. I told him from the bookstore, I wanted to open my own publishing company. He said to me, 'Dog you bigger than that. Why not just open the publishing company and then open the bookstore later?' I said, 'That's what it is.' He and I came together and bonded on the business aspect and opened up Real Edutainment Publishing together.

SWeT: So, that's your business partner?

JM: Yes, he encouraged me to shoot for the stars. Now Real Edutainment Publishing is a reality…

SWeT: And so is your bookstore. What's up with that and where is it located?

JM: With the assistance of Music N Motion, Real Edutainment Books was born. At this time, a variety of Urban Fiction is available, but as I get the love, support, and requests, I anticipate a variety of all genres.

SWeT: That's what's up. What would like to see for Real Edutainment in the future?

JM: I would like to see the company put out all quality work…impacting work, power stories, our people's stories. I would like to sign a host of talented authors, don't necessarily have to be African American authors, stories outside of hood tales cause that's not all we know and that's not all we're about. I just want a quality company with quality individuals. My reputation means more to me than the money because you can't buy a personality or a character. Anyone that's incarcerated and it's their dream or goal to become a published author, definitely I'm taking submissions. Somebody gave me a shot and I want to extend that same courtesy and that's my only reason for opening up my own publishing company. There was a publishing company that came out and was in a similar situation, came home from prison, got on, opened one of the largest African American publishing companies and used writers from in prison to become successful and rich but did nothing for our people. So, I want to create a company for the people. You can hit me up on my website. www.anewqualitypublishing.com (my new independent publishing company). You can catch me on myspace myspace.com/jmbenajmin_author.

SWeT: Oh ok. So, *My Manz and Em* is the first book published through Real Edutainment Publishing?

JM: Yeah *My Manz and Em*. The book industry is similar to the music industry. As long as u can produce the material you can sign as many deals as you want. I'm signed to Flowers in the Bloom publishing which put me out with *Down in the Dirty*. Now there's an anthology book called *Menace to Society* in which I contributed a story in there. That's under Melodrama Publishing. I signed a contract for that. I have my own publishing company, but if a major wanted to holla at me, like yo we'll give you X amount of dollars for a two book deal or a three book deal, if I could produce those books then I can sign that deal.

SWeT: Ok

JM: It doesn't conflict with any other obligations. As long as I can fulfill my obligations with anybody else, I can sign. I can do whatever I want in regards to the material. And it just so happens that I have 12 more manuscripts sitting in my closet so it's nothing if someone got at me and I threw them two books. Generally what happens is this. With *Down in the Dirty,* it came out. Right now, the majors are looking at me like damn this kid JM Benjamin just came out of nowhere. We keep hearing this Down in the Dirty book. We keep hearing about him. Let's see if he puts out another book and if he does, let's see if it does what the first one did. If it [does], somebody give him a call. So, like right now, when *My Manz and Em* drops that will solidify me as a consistent author or it could show that *Down in the Dirty* was all I had in me and my next one was a dud. I gotta go back to the lab. So, like I said with the music, same thing with the music. When you flop, you flop. You're only as good as your last hit.

SWeT: Exactly

JM: So I murdered them with *Down in the Dirty*. I'm trying to kill them with *My Manz and Em.* JM: Some of the authors that inspired me are now people that I interact with and deal with on a daily basis, personally, professionally all around the board which enabled me to open up my own company because just like in the music industry, knowledge is the key. If you don't know the business, bottom line, you already know the ending results. When I came home other authors, editors and publishers just instantly felt me and along the line everyone has given me valuable information free of charge, information that is not generally given out. I'm talking about the prices to get a book printed and binded, the most important things, that if you knew these answers, why would you need somebody else? You see what I mean. So it was just given to me because they said "Yo, this man deserves to be a boss. He doesn't need to be working for someone." You follow me?

SWeT: Yes

JM: Now a lot of authors that have been out longer than me reach out to me for advice and information. Like that's an honor for me. An author whose books I read while in prison…contacted me to ask me if I could give a review on the back of her book. I'm like "Damn, I seen some high powered authors on your last book that gave you reviews so you must view me in that light," so to me that's an honor. Like my favorite author wants to do a book with me now, the dude that inspired me to write.

SWeT: Ok

JM: So, you know, that's priceless for me. *Down in the Dirty* was nominated this year for Chicago Black Authors and Books awards [in May] so I'm trying to bring another home. It got nominated in 2 categories.

SWeT: That's what's up. Where can your book be purchased?

JM: Everywhere. You can catch my book in local beauty salons and barbershops. When *Down in the Dirty* came out, it came out 3 months before I came home so it came out prior to me touching. What I did was, the money that the publisher gave me in advance, I took that. Then, my brother matched that and we invested it in *Down in the Dirty* because as an author you are entitled to purchase your book at a low percentage. So, before I came home, my brother banged the hood with the books and he went to every beauty salon and barbershop in Plainfield. For the most part, they housed my books there free of charge, never charged me a dime and when I came home I offered them a cut of the books and they still turned it down. So, now that I have my own company and I can be a wholesaler, I afforded them the opportunity to invest in *My Manz and Em*. Rather than my books sitting in there and you push it, you will push more if you know that you profit. Business is business. So, what I'm doing now is allowing them to purchase the book from me at a wholesale price of $8 and sale it for $15. So, that's a $7 profit for them. I acknowledge all of them in my acknowledgments in my book and that's my way of showing them I appreciate that you appreciate me enough to support me so I'm just showing them that we gotta keep our money black. We gotta keep it within our community. We just gotta generate like everybody else. So even though I do signings at Barnes and Nobles, Borders and Walden's, there's nothing like doing them at black-owned stores, black entrepreneurial businesses. In a major store, I do 2-3 hour [signings]. In a black-owned store, I do 6-8 hours, sometimes 10 hours for a book signing. Why? Because so many African American bookstores go out of business because they can't compete with the majors...Because our people become successful as African American authors and don't go to the small mom and pop stores. Like D Block said, I'm not a industry dude I'm an in the streets dude so I keep it hood. I don't have to be in the hood to be hood. In a hood, where I come from, a hood is **your** hood. You're a family. So I'ma stay hood cuz I'm a family dude.

SWeT: What's the most important thing you would like readers to know about you?

JM: About me? Humility is the key to my success, because if I use emotion over intellect I'm not going to accomplish anything.

SWeT : Ok J. Thank you for your time.

After interviewing JM Benjamin it is obvious that he has a business as usual, go-getter type of attitude which his increasing success and popularity can also be attributed to. I was able to see him and his partner Kevin White schedule book signings, receive shipments of his book, and do a lot of foot work for their company *Real Edutainment Publishing*. JM Benjamin is real and has no problem with getting down and dirty for his success. He is dedicated to making it happen. He has been grinding, rain, sleet, heat, or snow, in the hood, in major book stores, in local mom and pop stores, and on the internet and most recently at *Real Edutainment Books*. That's right when he's not out doing book signings, doing speaking engagements or pushing his book, you may find him at *Real Edutainment Books*. He is making his name known…and ladies, he is single.

J.M Benjamin's success story is one that can be achieved simply by having your mind right, having confidence, and having the willingness and ambition to succeed. Know that for every door closed, there is another one opened. Stay focused. Never give up or limit yourself because everyone is capable of being successful if they want it bad enough. Everyone has a product whether it is writing, drawing, singing, dancing, producing, public/motivational speaking, etc. The only thing that you have to decide is what your product is, how to perfect it, and how to effectively market and sell it. Though it may be more difficult to achieve after convictions, as JM Benjamin has illustrated, success is always attainable. *So let's get it.*

Interview With SLR magazine (December 2008 issue)

By Erick S. Gray

Question: J.M. tell us a little about yourself?

Answer: I'm from Jersey, Plainfield, father of three, practically grew up in the streets, and served too much time in prison at a young age, but ironically it's where I discovered my talent and passion for writing.

Question: How long have you've been writing and what has the experience been like for you?

Answer: I've been writing novels since 2001. The experience for me was and still is very therapeutic, especially while I was still incarcerated and even now being home and living in an area not too far from where I grew up. Writing allowed me to channel my energy into something constructive and contributed to me finding humility, discipline, and just learning to focus and staying committed to something.

Question: What inspired your first book Down In The Dirty?

Answer: At the time I was reading tons of street novels, relating to them all because they were about where I came from and what I knew, but never really came across a story like Down In The Dirty, at least not told the way I told it. When I was in The Game back in the 80's, what the chicks were doing in my book was really going down, still is. I know a few dudes who lost their lives behind set ups, who went down to the dirty sleepin' on the south, thinkin' just because they were from up north they were sharper then the average. In my book, these women capitalized off of northern dudes arrogance and ignorance, and most of the times that's really what it was. Some chicks actually tried to get at me once upon a time, but wind up befriended me, and they really got down for theirs.

Question: What authors or novels do you admire most?

Answer: Hands down, I admire Claude Brown, who wrote ManChild In The Promised Land. How he over came his struggle, beating the odds, and battle with self, reminds me of myself. Then you have Donald Goines who, like myself, wrote his books while in prison. He was deep in the streets and captured them in their rawest form, that's what I try to do or would like to think that's what I do.

Question: Are your storylines based on a past experience?

Answer: Everything I write is in some way or another an experience of mine, either directly or indirectly. If I didn't do it or had it done to me then I know someone who has, did, or could do it. I write reality fiction, not Fantasy Island. When it comes to my writing, my imagination is but so vivid. It may sound far fetch to you, but it's my reality.

Question: Who are your all time favorite novel and or writer? Why?

Answer: My favorite author is James Paterson. The Alex Cross series got me thru my bids. It was a while before I even knew James Paterson wasn't a brother. They way he depicted an African American detective and maintained that character throughout his books was serious to me, and his ability to deceive the readers all the way to the end, that's what I'm into, deception stories, that makes for a ill plot. I incorporate some of his style into my own.

Question: What do you like best about being a writer?

Answer: My supporters. I love the impact that my work has on those who read it. The fact that I can entertain and educate a person at the same time means a lot to me. Words are powerful and I love the voice that I have in this field.

Question: What do you like to do on your free time?

Answer: What free time? I eat, sleep, and breathe this shit. I love doing what I do, that's what I do, move product everyday-all day. I went to prison for it, only difference, gotta new product and they aint given out no time for it. I do like movies and shows though so I squeeze those in.

Question: How do you feel abut this genre, the upcoming authors, and where you think its going?

Answer: Really, I think this genre is the best thing that happened to the hood in a long time. I own a book store, and I can tell you the Hood is readin'. Statically they say the reading percentage of our youth is low, but a lot of teenagers tell me my book or a friend of mines book was the first book they ever read and it had them wanting more. As for street lit authors, nowadays anybody can become an author, but its not everyone is a good story tellers, that's what's needed in this genre, like the Al-Saadiq Banks's, the K'Wan's, Treasure E. Blue's, Erick Gray's, Wahida Clark's, Ki Ki Swinson's, Kwame Teague's, Jason Poole's, T Syles, and shit, even the J.M.Benjamin's, and a lot more good story tellers. I feel we need more of us. No disrespect to anyone, but there's gonna come a time when you can't rely on your cover to move your book, gonna need some quality meat to feed the readers. Right now it's a free for all, but I believe structure will come into play in the near future because you do have some team players in the game and we over power those who have the

"Bigger Than" & "Better Than" mentality. Bottom line, this shit is here to stay!

Question: Growing up in Plainfield NJ, tell us what it was like growing up there?

Answer: It was like the movie New Jack City. I come from the Crack era, where our finest sisters beauty were stripped from them because of a drug, seen the thoroughest dude become the biggest coward because his heart was taken by a drug. I grew up seeing friends become foes over drugs. I watched my aunts, uncles, and father rob, steal, lie, sell, and con their way thru life over a drug. At 12, I was sucked in and swallowed up in the streets. There were no real dudes who I can say were positive role models in my hood that took the time out to say that's not right, or stay in school etc, so I followed what I saw and what was all around me. My pops hustled, robbed, etc, and his name rang bells in the streets. That does something to a kid. I'm just glad I'm able to be that role model in my town now that I didn't have growing up.

Question: Out of the many titles you've penned, which one do you hold close to your heart more, and why?

Answer: No doubt, the title My Manz And 'Em. That book is about a dude who grew up with the dudes he was getting paper with. When it came down to it, at the end of the day when shit gets thick you really find out who ya Manz And 'Em are. Not all who I thought my manz and 'em were really were. You learn that when you go to prison or if something pops off. Not everybody learns though so I wanted to educate those who know they going back out there as soon as the finish that bid. Through the main character Malik, I take you through the trials and tribulations a street dude goes through coming home wanting to do good but feeling that streets is all he knows. That character is a reminder to me, that's why I'm grateful for street lit, I don't know what I would be doing had it not been for this, maybe pushin' a different product still.

Question: What authors would you like to work with in the future and why?

Answer: Females I'd say T.Styles, Ki Ki Swinson, Wahida Clark, Nikki Turner, because they are the hardcore authors who are most consistent and I'm hardcore with mine so we'd get it in, and a few others. Dudes, Al-Saadiq, Kwan, Shannon Holmes, Erick Gray, Treasure, Kwame Teague, Caleb Alexander, really any dude that would like to work with me I'd like to work with, real talk.

Question: What goals do you have for yourself?

Answer: To put my children through college, buy my moms a house, leave enough paper for them for when I breathe my last breath, and stay out of jail while accomplishing all of it.

Question: What can we expect from you in the future?

Answer: Plenty. Just launched, along with a few partners, a new distribution company (www.alliancebookgroup.com) out in Mt. Vernon, 30 Lorraine Ave, also just launched a new independent publishing company, (A New Quality Publishing P.O.Box 589 Plainfield NJ 07061), look for Nyema's new book Back Stabbers, FiFi Cureton's Have You Ever, J-Rod Nider's Diamonds Are Forever, Stone Martin's Bullet Proof Love, and my joints On The Run With Love, Ride Or Die Chick 2, and Heaven & Earth. More info catch me on myspace.com/jmbenjamin_author or www.anewqualitypublishing.com.

Another View Bookshelf
JM Benjamin: Journey to Redemption

Tuesday, August 19, 2008 at 6:30 pm;
Rebroadcast Friday, August 22 at 11:30 pm

On this *Bookshelf* edition of *Another View* the compelling life of author JM Benjamin is profiled.

Benjamin grew up in the Second Street projects in Plainfield, New Jersey and saw the drug trade up-close and personal through his father and relatives. He began selling drugs at the age of 12, building a reputation as the 'go to' guy for crack cocaine. After spending a total of 12 years in prison, he now makes a living selling urban fiction based on his experiences in the drug trade.

It was a prison counselor at Fort Dix who encouraged Benjamin to write, giving him a journal where 400 pages of words flowed freely. With a new hustle, by the time he was released from prison, Benjamin authored "Down in the Dirty," and his name soon became popular in the 'free' world. Now, some 15,000 copies sold and two books later, the drug dealer turned author and publisher, shares his compelling story with *Another View*, about how he never writes a book where the bad guy gets away and how he almost lost his soul before his journey to redemption.

In The Projects (age 15)   In N.C. Prison (age 16)   In Federal Prison (age 31)

First Day Home   First Book Signing   The AAL Awards

  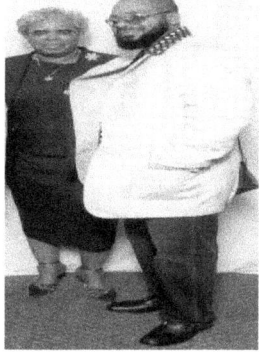

First television Interview   Out with Moms   2nd Book Release Party

108 FROM INCARCERATION 2 INCORPORATION

Visiting Father In Prison   **Visiting Me In Prison**

FROM INCARCERATION 2 INCORPORATION 109

Yaseena Easter "94"

Jamillah April "94"

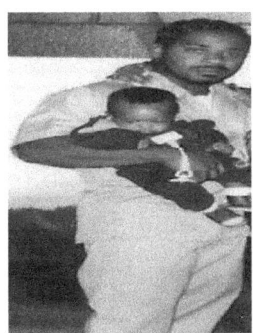
Jameel September "95"

Federal Prison "04"

Federal Prison "05"

3rd Novel Release Party "07"

First Visit w/ Son "06"

First Book Signing "06"

First Time Together "06"

Acknowledgements

First I'd like to thank The Almighty for guiding me and keeping me safe through this journey and process of change and also allowing me the strength and knowledge of information to share a great deal of my story with you all. I'd like to acknowledge and thank those who inspired and gave me the ammunition to write this passage of my past, present and as to date future, my parents, my siblings, my children, my friends, my foes, etc, each of you all have served a purpose through-out my life for whatever reason, and through you all I have learned many valuable lessons. A special thanks to my friend Randy Kearse for coming up with this concept and believing enough in me to say I was the only worthy candidate in his book he felt could deliver what he was looking for in this motivational piece. Like minds indeed came together in this one And lastly, I 'd like to thank each and every last one of you who has taken the time out to read this book from cover to cover. It is my deepest hope that you receive this message the way it was delivered and embrace it with all your heart and strength then pass it on to another, then another, and another so they may also do the same.

Peace,

J.M.Benjamin

Plain Talker

Your source for news since June 2005

J.M. Benjamin Interview Online
If you missed Tuesday's NJN interview with Plainfield author **J.M. Benjamin**, you can see it online here for a while. It will also be on NJN Channel 23 on Comcast at 11:30 p.m. Friday (Jan. 18, 2008).

In a city where hundreds of parolees come home each year, J.M. Benjamin is a good example of how to make positive, life-changing decisions. In the interview, he cites a book by **Randy Kearse**, "Changin' Your Game Plan," that offers a way to use incarceration for redemption.

Among Plainfield's very diverse population, a significant number of people are dealing with issues of incarceration or having a family member or loved one incarcerated. It's easy to dismiss people who made bad choices, but these individuals are our neighbors and need our acknowledgement and encouragement to find new ways to make money and rejoin the community.

Thanks to J.M. Benjamin for telling us how he learned to make new choices.

--Bernice Paglia

Other titles by J.M. Benjamin

To Order: autograph copies www.anewqualitypublishing (paypal), A New Quality Publishing P.o.box 589 Plainfield New Jersey 07061. copies www.amazon.com, www.alliancebookgroup.com, or wherever books are sold!

FROM INCARCERATION TO INCORPORATION

The Rise, Fall, and Rise Again of Randy Kearse

"There are no failures, just quitters."

Russell Simmons

Author's Background

Born: December 17, 1964 (9lbs 10 oz.), Brooklyn Hospital

Parents: Beverly and Allan Kearse

Siblings: Tracy, Francine, Dennis (DK), Stephen, Lonnie, Jamal (Goobie)

Raised: Brooklyn, NY (Farragut Houses)

School: P.S. 170, McKinley JHS, Fort Hamilton H.S. (Expelled) Eastern District H.S. (a.k.a. E.D. a.k.a. Educated Dummies) dropped out. An above average student throughout school Randy became bored with school. He ditches the books for the working world. (Acquired GED without studying or taking classes to prepare).

First Job: age 17 Minute Men Messenger Service.

First Arrest: April 1982 (For attempted murder which resulted in his first trip to Rikers Island (Adjudicated youthful offender)

First prison sentence: September 1984 (4 months and 6 months probation). Upon his release Randy tried to stay out of trouble, his Uncle Coleman secured him a good job in the garment district and things were looking promising.

Fathered first child: Age 20 (young and irresponsible).

1986 – Walking the tight rope of doing the right thing and running the streets, Randy would eventually get caught up in the whirl wind of the crack epidemic. The lure of making fast money would make him jump head first into the grimy bowels of the illegal drug trade. Using his book smarts and his street sense he would rise to the higher ranks of known drug dealers from Brooklyn. With his partners in crime (names better left out) they hustled their way from the mean streets of Brooklyn to the too sweet and ripe state of North Carolina. At the height of his hustle, Randy and his team were 25 deep and spread across three cities.

1992 – After a long 6 year run, like the song says, "When you dance to the music – you have to pay to the piper." Randy was wanted in the same three cities he once flooded with mayhem and chaos. The Feds, the DEA, the New York City and the Raleigh Police were looking for and gunning to bring him and his cohorts in to dance that last dance. They say it's not over until the fat lady sings; well the fat lady was waiting in the wings for the day Randy was brought before her.

April 1992 – Randy was captured in Chapel Hill NC

October 1992 - Randy received 15 years in Greensboro NC

November 1992 – The Prison Journey began.....

August 17, 2005 – Randy was released after serving 13 years, 6 months and 2 days in Federal Prison. A changed man with a new game plan....

Like Minds Come Together

Date: Early 2005.

Finding a true friend in prison is like finding the proverbial needle in a haystack. Then sometimes a true friend finds you. I can count on one hand the number of people that I had considered a true friend over the years. A friend who'd give you his last, or who didn't hide behind the false facades and personas that many men in prison cloak themselves in, who wasn't afraid to tell you when you were wrong, and admit when you were right. I think I'm a very good judge of character; at least I try to be. There were those few occasions where I misread someone and extended my hand in friendship and wound up regretting it. Real friendships are rare in prison.

After 13 years in prison my friendship committee was all but shut down. I had been in a federal correctional facility in NJ called Fort Dix for 5 years now and I stayed to myself. Most the guys in Fort Dix were just starting their time and I just didn't have the patience to deal with the issues that establishing friendship brings. I just wanted to go home. I was cool just blending in and staying out the way. The few people who I did socialize with I either knew me from the streets or I had met them through the course of my time in prison. In prison you learn to be leery when it comes to befriending someone.

In prison, staying to yourself and not getting caught up in the prison culture or the politics of prison can make you stand out a lot more then you intend to. People like me are like anomaly in prison. I had been working on my first book "Street Talk" for close to five years now and this project consumed most of my time. If I was known for anything within the prison it would have to be for my determination to make Street Talk a publishable manuscript. I could talk to you for hours about publishing and my dream to get a book published.

Because people couldn't figure me out, most came to the conclusion that I was bugged out; not mentally sound I guess you can say. Another term used when referring to me was "burnt out". I didn't watch TV unless it was news or informational. I didn't play sports and I didn't sit around indulging in frivolous conversation. So that pretty much left me to myself most the time. I was on a mission, and to understand that you had to be on a mission as well.

I've listened to my fair share of grandiose plans brothers had for themselves only to observe through their behaviors most didn't possess the necessary discipline, determination and passion to see those plans all the way through no matter what.

There are times in our lives that are marked by significant moments and significant events, like when I was able to get a literary agent to represent me and my work while I was still inprison. A profound moment for me that will always be a marker in my life would be the day I met JM Benjamin. A true friend, brother, and comrade.

JM and I were introduced by a mutual acquaintance named Ali. Ali was one of those type of brothers who knew everything and everybody. He was into everything in the jail. Me and Ali lived in the same housing unit so he pretty much knew what I was about. He had been incarcerated over a decade or so like me. So he pretty much understood my standoffish ways when it came to people. Ali worked in the barber shop so he stayed abreast of the daily goings-on within the prison. So it was kind of strange when one day I heard Ali was looking for me. I knew we had no beef so that was removed from thought immediately; I didn't owe'em any money so that was erased just as quickly, so my curiosity got the best of me. I made it my business to find Ali. When I was finally able to track him down he told he had a brother named Mustafa that he wanted me to meet. Mustafa like me was a writer. Mustafa was his Muslim name, and JM Benjamin was his birth and pen name.

From the time Mustafa and I met we bonded instantly. Our first conversation centered on writing and publishing with both of us eager to learn what the other one had learned. After a couple hours of discussion we agreed to meet the next day in the library and bring our writings and the publishing information we had been gathering. The next day we met, I produced a 1,000 page manuscript that was pretty impressive; Mustafa on the other hand produced several different manuscripts that he had written. From that day forward we would meet in the library during the day and walk the yard in the evenings. We talked out about our plans to take the literary world by storm and if we weren't welcomed with open arms we'd use a lil strong arm tactics.

JM was the total opposite of me on the surface, but in heart and mind we could have been twins. JM made his presence known as soon as he arrived on the prison compound. After a week he was walking around the joint like he'd been there 5 years. Me on the other hand, you'd have to ask several different people who I was, what housing unit I lived in and what I looked like before people could put two and two together and figured out who you were talking about. By first impression one would assume I was a nerd or square and I liked it just like that.

Before you know it, JM had connected with every aspiring writer within the prison. He'd have writing projects for guys, discussions around writing and publishing, and he'd never withhold information or a potential contact from anyone. What struck me about this brother was his self assurance that when the time came he was going to make a name for himself in the publishing industry. A humble brother, but very confident and that's how I was.

Our meeting was destiny; like minds coming together to script a blueprint of success for brothers and sisters to follow in prison or not.

We both came from the streets, we never held long talks about our past exploits, and there was no need to. All our talks centered around the future not the past. We were looking at life from a perspective of what we planned to do not what we already did by the time we met. We were already removed from the ritual story telling brothers have when trying to prove themselves as being tough, thug, or a "real" drug dealer.

I had no problem telling JM when he made it big to put me on his back and carry me up the ladder of success. True friends don't care who makes it first as long as the other one opens the door of success.

I was released several months before JM and we stayed in constant contact when I made it home. He was there to encourage me as I struggled to re-build my life and lay the ground work for our book publishing plans. After I secured the publishing deal for Street Talk ninety days after my release, he pushed me to complete, Changin' Your Game Plan.

Our friendship transcends what we do for a living, and is embedded in what we are doing with our lives, for our community and for our families. JM is and has always been a man of great integrity.

By the time you finish this book you'll understand why I have nothing but respect, love, and admiration for Brother JM Benjamin.

Introduction from Randy Kearse

This book comes on the 3rd anniversary of my freedom. In September 2005, I was released from federal prison. I had served 13 years, 6 months and 2 days on a 15 year sentence. Because of the harsh sentencing laws enacted in the 1990's and the abolishment of the federal parole system I had to serve 85% of the sentence rendered. The purpose of this book is to chronicle my journey "From Incarceration to Incorporation". My journey is not solely about where I am today, but how I got to be where I am today; a bestselling author, business owner, motivational speaker, and entrepreneur. My journey has been filled with a lot of pain, a lot of suffering (for the most part I caused myself) because of the lifestyle I chose to live. Almost twenty years separates my dark past and my bright present and brighter future, but no matter how much time passes there is always residue from the past that I have to deal with. Bad choices made, irresponsible decisions, and a reckless disregard for anyone but me is something that time cannot erase. My journey has also been filled with failures and triumphs, setbacks as well as accomplishments that have exceeded my wildest expectations. My life has been just that, a journey, filled with challenges and struggles. A journey I continue to travel as each day passes.

I have met so many people during this, at times, tumultuous journey called life. A collage of faces that I carry with me every day and everywhere I go. Family and friends who have passed away way too soon, friends who have traveled different roads then I, never to see what had become of them. Friends I shared a smile, a laugh and at times a cry with. Friends I shared my dreams with, and who never judged me when I fell short of reaching for those dreams. The many faces of friends who fill the inside of city, state, and federal prisons, faces I probably will never see again.

This book is dedicated to the collage of faces who have played a part in my journey of life, no how matter how brief the encounter, no matter how fleeting the moment, no matter how insignificant it may have seemed at the time, these people have left their footprints in the sand of my memory. The collage of faces I carry around with me has helped keep me going during my darkest moments. Standing at the brink of hopelessness and surrounded by the fog of despair, there were times in my life that I honestly didn't know how I was going to make it. My mother often told me to pray, but for me, with all the wrong I had done I felt that I was beyond being saved by prayer alone.

The list of names is long, the memories even longer.

Wherever you are, whatever you are doing, please know that I could have never made it through the darkest part of my journey without you. When you see me on TV, read an article about me in a newspaper, magazine, or on the internet, have a smile on me. When you hear my voice coming through the radio turn that radio up, and tell anyone within earshot that you know me. Be proud of me, but more importantly be proud that as a Blackman I am carrying on the tradition of other Black men who have fallen in life only to rise to be stronger, wiser, and resolute.

Some of you have witnessed me at my worst and still believed there was something good inside of me. Some of you believed in me when I didn't know how to believe in myself. Some of you taught me how to look ahead and not back. Thank you and I carry your faces with me forever.

P.S.

If you read my book, **Changin' Your Game Plan: *How to use incarceration as a stepping stone for SUCCESS***, you know I dropped a lot of powerful life lessons and deep thought provoking nuggets to better one's life. In this book it was my intention to give the reader a glimpse of who I used to be and the lifestyle I used to live in order to show the reader who may have a similar story as mines what he/she can accomplish if they decide to change their game plan.

In order to know who I am today, you have to know who I was yesterday because I wasn't always this positive individual you see today. We sometimes have to visit our past for people to understand out present and foresee our future.

I'm not proud of the life I used to live, but if not for the journey that I have traveled in this life I wouldn't and couldn't be the person I am today. So the question that begs to be answered is…. Would I change anything about my past if I had an opportunity to? And the answer is this, if I could change anything about my past it would be this…. I would be a better son to my mother, a better father to my children, and a better friend to my true friends.

(Article excerpted from the Discovery Channel website http://investigation.discovery.com/investigation/where-now/kearse/kearse.html)

Ex-Con on a Mission: The Randy Kearse Story

Research has shown that one out of every four prison inmates will return to prison within one to three years of his or her release, a phenomenon that does not say much for the rehabilitative effects of incarceration. Some blame the prison system, while others blame the inmates themselves for lacking the motivation to get on the straight and narrow. Regardless of who is at fault for the high rate of recidivism, however, one exception to the common pattern is Randy Kearse, an ex-con who chose to follow a different path.

Randy grew up in the Farragut housing projects in Brooklyn, N.Y. From the time he was young, Randy's parents tried to instill positive values in their son, hoping he would not stray from them as so often happens with those who grow up in the projects. They taught him the importance of education, and with their encouragement he did well in school. However, by age 17 things began to change. Bored with his studies, Randy desired a new outlet for his creativity and energy. Unfortunately, like so many others from his area, Randy turned his attention to selling drugs.

It was the lure of fast money that drew him. Crack cocaine was the drug of choice during the late 1980s and early '90s, and there was no shortage of addicts desperate to buy it. Unlike most drug dealers, Randy did not become a regular user himself. He realized from the start that a dealer couldn't make much money if he became dependent on his own product. Instead, he stuck to dealing, and within a short time his operation grew to encompass three South Carolina cities. By then, he had assembled a gang of 25 men who helped him traffic the drug, pulling in an estimated $100,000 per month. Randy would later say that the money came in so fast it was hard to keep up with how much he was making.

Randy's success as a drug dealer was destined to be short-lived. Few can play the game without getting caught, and in 1992, Randy was arrested for trafficking in crack cocaine. During his subsequent trial, the judge called him a "menace to society" and sentenced him to 15 years in a federal prison for conspiracy to distribute narcotics.

Unlike many inmates who choose to blame the system for their situation, rather than themselves for having landed in prison, Randy was profoundly affected by his conviction. The disappointment he saw on his mother's face cut him deeply. At 27 years old, he was beginning to understand the wisdom his parents had tried to pass down to him, and once again he began to value his mother's moral code.

On the day Randy began serving his sentence, another inmate was murdered, and this incident troubled him deeply. Not long after, a good friend and fellow drug dealer of Randy's was tortured and murdered. These two events were an eye-opener for Randy, and they strengthened his resolve to make a better life for himself. He did not want to become another statistic.

During his incarceration, Randy was struck with an inspiration when he observed another inmate with a book titled 1,001 Jokes. As he flipped through the pages, an idea began to form in his mind, and he decided to set about writing his own book about 1,001 street slang expressions. After all, material for the book was readily available, considering that Randy was locked up with people from coast to coast and thus had access to regional slang from all over the country. Randy also had contact with inmates from different generations, which gave his list a historical flair. In fact, Randy's goal was easily met, and what had started as a project including 1,001 expressions soon turned into 10,001.

It took Randy seven years to complete his book project, and he was released from prison shortly thereafter, in 2005. Afterward, with the financial backing of his mother, Randy kept true to his dream and self-published the book STREET TALK: Da Official Guide to Hip-Hop & Urban Slanguage. He then sold it to Barricade Books, an independent publisher, who was able to distribute it to bookstores around the world. Excited by his newfound success, Randy quickly followed up with a second book, Changin' Your Game Plan! How to Use Incarceration as a Stepping Stone for SUCCESS.

Randy's second book has proved to be an inspiration to others and has helped many inmates make positive changes in their lives. In this book, Randy uses his own life story to inspire and teach. He does not focus solely on physical incarceration, but includes chapters on mental confinement as well. According to Randy, the purpose of the book is to reach out to youth, to show them the danger of heading down the same road he took. He writes passionately as he explains how to turn a negative situation into a positive one. In addition, he exposes what he refers to as the "game" and the ways in which people get caught up in it, preventing them from reaching their true potential.

Today, Randy is the president of Positive Urban Literature Inc., a company dedicated to promoting positive images within the African-American community. Randy continues to sell his books and often takes to the road as a motivational speaker at seminars and speaking engagements around the country. Randy has appeared on Comedy Central's Colbert Report, Tyeartv, and various other television and radio programs. In addition, Slate.com, the London Guardian,

Brooklyn Courier and a plethora of Web sites have sought him out for interviews.

Randy has also taken advantage of the Internet by creating Myprisonjournal.com, a Web site giving those locked behind bars a venue for speaking out about issues that concern them. It also serves as a forum for ex-cons to teach and inspire as Randy has done.

Randy Kearse took what, for many, would have been an insurmountable hurdle and turned it into an opportunity. He found a way to make his mistakes pay off, and in doing so he has helped reach others who find themselves in similar situations. While Randy is certainly in the minority — a driven and successful ex-con — he continues to work hard to help others.

Success is 90 percent attitude, and 10 percent aptitude."

Unknown

From Good to Hood(lum)

(Had anyone told me back in the days that I'd travel some of the roads I've traveled so far in this life, I would've told them they were crazy. I doubt if anyone growing up aspires to be a criminal. I was like many of young black men growing up with dreams. My dream was to be a teacher, follow in the footsteps of my mother. I was an above average student all through school, but became bored in high school and felt there was nothing else I needed to learn. Cutting class, playing hooky, and running behind the girls was more fun (sound familiar?). I'd skip school days at a time, until I eventually stopped going altogether (sound familiar?). Outta five brothers and one sister I was the only one who didn't graduate from high school.

When my moms realized she couldn't force me to go to school, she allowed me to stop going on two conditions: 1. I had to get a job. 2. I had to get my GED (which she arranged for me to take, and I passed easily, without even studying).

Dropping out of school was the first of a long list of bad decisions I've made in my life. Choices that I regret to this day. I thought hanging out with the so-called cool crowd was the thing. Not realizing that the cool people were really the ones going to school every day getting their education.

My mother tried her best to give her kids the tools they would need out in the world. She emphasized education, working hard and staying out of trouble. Though my pops lived in the crib with us, he was often distant. It was as if we grew up without him. Moms was the one who tried to school us on what to expect out there in the streets. No matter how many times someone tells you something; sometimes you have to learn the hard way in order to understand what they were telling you.

From 16 to 21 yrs. old, I walked a fine line between doing the right thing and getting into trouble. I worked every day and I

did my share of dirt too. I caught a 4 month prison sentence during that period for stabbing a guy at a skating rink. The stabbing was the result of a long running beef I had with some guys from Queens. When I came home from doing the 4 months, I went right back to working (my uncle Coleman saw to it that I got my job back). At a time when a lot of my friends were catching cases (for robbery) and going up state, I continued to walk that fine line between right and wrong (freedom and jail).

It wouldn't be until the mid eighties when I'd forget about doing the right thing and completely go the wrong route. It was in the very early days of, what would later be called the 'crack epidemic', that I jumped head first into the vile world of the drug trade. If you didn't know me or the way I was raised, you would have thought I was raised to be nothing more than the drug dealer I had become.

The so-called game became my life, the only thing I lived to do. I traded in my childhood dreams, for the dream of being a successful drug lord. I traded in my friends who lived the straight and narrow, for the grimy, untrustworthy, and shady characters you run with in the streets. For the love of the money I became enemies with childhood friends and forged alliances with people I had little or no history with.

In five years, I went from standing on the corner hustling for myself to being one half of a drug network that reached from New York to North Carolina. Me and my partner in crime (May he rest in peace) reached the highest ranks of ghetto super-stardom. We made and spent money like there was no tomorrow. You couldn't tell us we hadn't made it. The future for us was, waiting for the next time to split our illegal profits and re-up with the next drug shipment. To us our plan was flawless. We had been getting away for so long, getting caught only happened to the other people.

The higher you climb the criminal ladder in the streets, the further you fall. When everything began to come crashing down around me, life began to feel like the feeling you get when you're gasping for air in the midst of drowning. I had already done too much dirt to walk away, so I continued to play the so-called game to my last breath.

All the years I had refused to consider the serious consequences of my actions, made the inevitable feel like I had been hit in the head with a ton of bricks. It was no longer dismissing thoughts of what might happen if I got caught, now there was a sense of dread of what was gonna happen when I got caught. The only thing I was living for now was, staying one step ahead of being arrested. I was on the run.

My reign as a ghetto celebrity/drug dealer ended like a low budget bootleg movie. The same ghetto celeb who had once stayed in five star hotels and ate at five star restaurants was now hiding out in a roach infested welfare hotel (the one that doesn't have a phone in the room and you have to wear flip flops in the shower). Excerpted from Changin' Your Game Plan, By Randy Kearse

When you're young you don't consider the consequences of your actions. You think you'll either live forever or die young. This is the mentality of the streets. I was a victim of this mentality. Where did I get it from? I adopted it because it damn sure wasn't taught at home. I adopted it, because it made feel alive. It made me feel like I was in control of something. I remember being scared to death before I committed a crime or acted out some random act of violence, but I also remember thinking that if I didn't participate in this wrong behavior how it would affect how my peers looked at or received me. In an environment where you're constantly being told only the strong survive, the last thing you wanted to be perceived as was being weak in the streets.

There are parts of my story that are too dark and too painful to tell. I'm only choosing to share my journey with you so maybe some other young person doesn't have to go through what I went through. Doesn't have to spend a good portion of their life before they figure out the street life is a road to prison or the graveyard, with a lot of pain and suffering along the way to the final destination.

There's no glory or badge of honor for being a thug or drug dealer. I'm not trying to justify my past wrong doings because there is no justification for the life I chose to live. What I hope to do is to explain my past in a way that makes it clear to anyone who's caught up in the maze of the streets how easily it is to lose everything when you think you have everything to gain chasing the illusions of street success.

My story isn't one of those stories that are made up of hardships growing up as a child. It isn't a story that one might automatically assume I was destined to become the person who would do a lot of the things that I did in this life. It's a story of a young person who for most his young life yearned for attention, acceptance and self gratification. It's a story about a Black youngster who could have been anything and done anything with his life. I was smart enough to go college, but didn't see college as a place I wanted to be. My story is the story of many young Black men.

I fell victim to my wants and my wants lead me down a road of self destruction. I tossed out every sense of right and surrounded myself with everything that was wrong, mentally and morally. I wanted my piece of the American dream but unlike my mother and father, I didn't want to work or struggle for it. I was part of a new generation who wanted what they wanted and when they wanted it.

Don't get me wrong I once believed in the concept of working hard, I'm NOT one of those people who say, "I never worked a day in my life". I did the working 9-5 thing, but down in my heart I knew it wasn't something I wanted to do for the rest of my life.

I always saw myself doing something big with my life. Never knew quite what it would be, but from a young age I had an entrepreneur spirit. I know it's difficult for some people to rationalize selling drugs as being entrepreneurial but in its simplest essence it is. Many young black men like me gravitated toward selling drugs because we seen and seized on an opportunity to make money in spite of it being at the expense of other people's weakness to consume drugs. That's what entrepreneurs do. They see an opportunity and they move in to seize upon it. When one truly posses an entrepreneurial spirit it doesn't die when a venture or investment fails. Just the opposite happens, it re-ignites his or her entrepreneurial spirit and that person moves on to scout for the next big project. Entrepreneurs spend a good sum of their life going from one project to another trying to find that one or two or three successful ventures that will allow them to be the independent force he or she is.

I started making enough money in drugs that I now looked at working as something suckers did, and during one of those arrogant selfish and shameful moments during my false sense of being successful I even told my mother that working was for suckers even though she got up every day and went to work. I think I said something like, "I'm not working for twenty years just to get a gold watch, when I can buy my gold watch now". (My mother long since retired often brings up this moment in our sometimes tumultuous past relationship and then alludes to the fact that she got her gold watch, two cars paid for, property and ability to do whatever the heck she wants to all because she chose to work).

A lot of us got blinded by the money that was in front of us and the status it brought. For us this was going to get us everything we wanted in life without the necessary hard work and sacrifices that needed to be made.

Looking Back

Life is funny sometimes when you look back. I remember sitting in my living room one long ago day (1990's) when I used to hustle aka sell drugs and here it was, I was sitting in front of the TV counting my illegal profits, a HBO documentary called The Big House was playing on the TV. The documentary centered on the infamous Lewisburg Federal penitentiary and those who were unfortunately housed there. As I here sit today (2008) chronicling my journey from incarceration to incorporation, again, I find it ironic that this memory is so profound because I would eventually end up in the Lewisburg penitentiary about two years later. In a way out wacky kind of way I wonder if some of the people in the documentary were watching me from within the TV as I halfass paid attention to them, as I was more concerned about counting my illegal drug profits then what was going on with them. Were they trying to warn me, laughing at me or shaking their heads knowing where I'd eventually end up?

The reason I went to prison is simple... greed and lust for the money as well as the ghetto celebrity status that having large amounts of money brings. I was drunk off being revered, respected and sometimes feared in the hood. So flashing back to the scene where I'm counting money in the living room and the Lewisburg documentary is playing, I'm sure I probably made some naive comment to myself or at the TV itself, probably in regards to the individuals in the documentary and how they probably messed up or slipped up in some way which landed them in prison. It would take me to walk in their shoes to understand the politics behind so many African Americans being in prison.

Before I get into my journey of incarceration, let me go back to how I landed in federal prison in the first place. I promise not to blame it on the system, my environment, my upbringing, or the white man. Maybe some of these things had a hand in my incarceration; the ultimate reason for my incarceration is mines and mines alone. The roles these things did play pale in comparison to the role I played myself that caused my incarceration.

****

It was 1990, the height of what is now known as the crack era. For those of us who were selling and dealing drugs it was a cash filled era like never before. Money was all over the streets. For those who were using the drugs it was a hurricane that would sweep their lives away. Hurricane Crack; Dreams were lost, families destroyed and many lives lost. Children were abandoned and/or left to fend for themselves. But who had time to care? All the drug dealers concerned about was making more money, expanding more territory and spending their ill gotten gains. We stayed dipped in the latest fashions, drove the hottest cars, ate at the best restaurants. The way we saw it, we were ghetto capitalist, capitalizing on other people's needs to get high. One of the rationales that you'd often hear us use was, "if I don't sell it to them someone else would".

Home base for me was Brooklyn NY. A nine building public housing complex named Farragut Houses. I was born and raised here. In the hustling days of old, you had the old timers saying "you never shit and eat in the same place", meaning that you didn't commit crime close to where you lived. In this new era of hustling, many of those principals were thrown slam out the window. You secured your home turf and then if you were bold enough and strong enough you set out to make your mark in other areas of your city or in cities of other states aka going o.t. (outta town) to spread your hustle.

As someone who always possessed an entrepreneurial spirit, getting into selling drugs was only a natural transition. I was working a decent job when the crack epidemic was ushered in. I was working as a shipping clerk making whatever minimum wages was back then, two dollars thirty five cents I think. Had my own lil bachelor pad, things were good for me.

My first attempt to delve into selling crack was a light hearted move. I brought way too little amount of cocaine, maybe like an 8 ball, to do any serious drug selling. I then had the neighborhood drug chemist cook the cocaine it into crack (which was actually called base, the name crack wouldn't come until later). This amateur attempt was a waste of time because I didn't even get back enough product to make my money back. I was a drug dealer for about two hours selling what lil product I had to the people who were hanging out in the drug chemist's house. This was discouraging but it was also a learning experience. It would be a couple months later that I'd really begin to make my mark in the world of crack dealing. Me and my brother DK who'd been recently released from prison teamed up the next time I'd try my hand at dealing drugs. We found it easier, faster, and more profitable to travel to Washington Heights and purchase already cooked up vials of crack at wholesale prices, bring it back to the projects and then sell the vials retail. This proved to be a winning formula for awhile. Sometimes we'd find a steady wholesaler that we'd deal with on a regular basis, and sometimes we'd go uptown shopping looking for the best product and cheapest prices. The neighborhood crackheads would love when it was time for us to go shopping for new product. Those who were lucky enough to be chosen to go, it meant they would get to test aka smoke up a lot of crack during the quest to find new quality product.

This time the stage was being set for my climb up in drug trade underworld. Things got so good that me and DK would take on my oldest brother Tracy as a partner. Then we went and recruited the most well liked crackhead in the projects, Deb. Everybody had a role to play, me and DK watched over Deb as she sole bags of crack for what seemed like all of 24 hrs. We'd take turns keeping her safe, while Tracy's job was to make the trips uptown to Washington Heights to purchase the drugs from the wholesale drug connection we were able to secure. This was a winning formula.... for a while that is.

As with any successful business with multiple partners, everyone wanted to be the boss. Everybody had a different answer to every problem that came up, so eventually nerves wore thin and we all wound up doing our different drug dealing things. DK wound up keeping Deb with him, now a re-formed crackhead who completely stopped using drugs, Deb became a powerhouse hustler. Me and Tracy teamed up for a minute. With me shouldering most of the responsibilities because Tracy worked a fulltime job, our partnership slowly wore thin and I eventually went on to do my own drug dealing thing. Hell if I had to go get it, standout there and sell it I mineaswell get all the profit, I was taking all the risk.

Things were good for me. I wasn't making anywhere as much drug money as DK and Deb, but I did ok. It wouldn't be until I teamed up with an outsider that I would take my drug dealing capabilities to higher heights. The reason I termed this person an outsider is because this person didn't grow up in the projects like me. By the time he moved to the projects friendships were already solidified from childhood. So even though he and his family moved into the same building that I lived in, he was looked at as an outsider. His name was (of course I have to change the name, not to protect the innocent, because there were innocent on my side of the story but to protect my butt from being sued) Mike.

As probably typical of any teenager moving into a new neighborhood there were eventual conflicts that arose because Mike was the new kid in the building. Normal beefs, like words passed or people feeling they had to prove themselves. Soon the conflicts subsided and people got used to Mike the outsider. Some people accepted him and a lot of people didn't. Most people who didn't like him didn't trust him. They always felt that his loyalty did not lay in the new formed friendships made when he moved to the projects, but more aligned with the friends he'd grown up with and who would often come visit him.

It was a shocking surprise to everyone who knew me when I announced that I was taking the outsider Mike on as a partner. DK pulled me aside one day and said if Mike ever crossed me he was gonna kill'em. And there were likewise comments whispered to the outsider Mike about me from his friends I'm sure. Family and friends on both sides of our newly formed team were leery of the other one.

Over time though people came to accept and respect the friendship the outsider Mike and I formed. Of course some still harbored distrust on both sides but it wasn't as strong as it had been in the beginning.

Mike knew nothing about selling drugs. He'd often tell people later that I taught him everything he knew about drug dealing. He went from being a student to being a teacher in no time and in no time we climbed the ladder of accomplished drug dealers in Brooklyn. We were one of the few neighborhood dealers who'd open up drug spots outside of the projects. We wouldn't keep them long but we would open up shop anywhere, earning us the nickname, the "drug dealing gypsies". After several months of selling drug from spot to spot we finally decided to bring our show home to the projects. DK and Deb were making a killing by this time, so it only made sense that we go home.

Only thing was we had a going home plan that we knew not everyone in the projects would totally agree with, you know the saying, "get down or lay down". We were coming back to the projects with that mentality. Our push was going to be a slow methodically push to stake our claim to the top half of the projects. DK and Deb already had the most clientele at the top of the projects, but there were just too many stragglers. When Mike and I stepped to DK and Deb about the plan they were all for it, it meant more paper for them and a sense of strength that all drug dealers needed to survive the drug world. Mike and I set up shop in a building across from DK and Debs operation. We sold dope, coke, crack and weed out the apartment 24 hours a day 7 days a week. We slowly started amassing an arsenal of weapons and a crew that would be a force to be reckoned with. We acquired two Israeli Uzi submachine guns, numerous handguns, automatic shotguns, bullet proof vest (police issued at that). We pretty much were ready for anything.

It was New Years Eve 1988, and as a tradition, all the guns and gunmen from the projects would make their way up to the rooftops of their respective buildings and at the stroke of midnight all guns would blaze. Up until now no one from the projects knew what kind of heat we were holding and tonight we were planning to make a statement for the whole projects to hear. We'd do things a little different than everyone else this night, we'd wait to after the midnight toll, let everyone else fire their weapons, and then when all shots went silent we would let loose a fuselage of gunfire. Just like we planned, when it was our turn to fire our weapons we did so in unison. Rrrrr, Rrrrr, Rrrrr, Boom, Boom, Boom, Rrrrr, Rrrrr that's all you heard. It sounded like a mini war, the smell of gunpowder filled the immediate air and spent shells littered the ground. When our guns finally fell silent we all had smiles on our faces. We bagged up the guns and sent them to the safe house. Me, DeeKay, Mike, Sam, Puerto Rock, Sha and the other gunmen we had with us all walked up the block where Deb was waiting for us in front of her building. Deb, being the loud boisterous female she could be was bragging and boasting and telling anyone within earshot that there were some new sheriffs in town.

As with every story in the 'hood, the story about the gunfire on the roof of 224 took on a life of its own. Some say you could hear the gunshots all the way in the next projects, some said the gunfire lasted 10 minutes without interruption, some say the shots were fireworks designed to fool people into thinking we had that kind of fire power. Whatever the case, those who needed to know, now knew we had the heavy arms to bring the pain.

Farragut projects sat a few blocks from an infamous project named Fort Greene. Fort Greene gave birth to some of Brooklyn's most notorious stickup kids; 50 cents (not the rapper), Killer Ben, the Lugo Brothers, D Whiz and Itru just to name a few. From I guess time can remember Farragut and Fort Greene projects kept beef. As drug money flowed in abundance in Farragut, the stickup kids from Fort Greene would pay regular visits to Farragut to relieve drug dealers of their illegal gains.

Once me and my people were ready to make the play for the top part of the projects we had been planning all along, we put the word out to all the straggler drugs dealers who were selling in front of the buildings we had our spots in, they could no longer stand in front of those buildings and sell because they weren't ready to protect, kill or even be killed holding the projects down against the stickup kids from Fort Greene. To make our point perfectly clear we offered a show down with anyone who was in disagreement with what we were saying. The night of the showdown we brought out the big guns and waited for whoever wanted it. No one showed.

I guess you could say we were expressing our entrepreneurial spirits with the moves we were making. In the corporate world what we were doing would be called a hostile takeover, only ours was literal.

We made a lot of enemies within our own 'hood during the push. Childhood friends became hateful of us. Most questioned how we could stop anyone who lived in the projects from selling in the projects, but that wasn't the case…. All we said was that you couldn't sell at the top half of the projects.

Then we put the word out to the stickup kids from Fort Greene in no uncertain terms, that if you get caught trying to rob any of our spots or our workers at the top part of Farragut projects that you play at your own risk.

It wouldn't be long before we'd make an example out an infamous stickup kid named Doe from Gawanus Projects. Doe came around one late winter night asking questions about DeeKay and Deb's operation, questions that only a stickup kid would ask when they're scheming on a robbery. Word made its way to DeeKay and Deb who in turn notified me and Mike. When we got the code red call we immediately strapped up and went downstairs to investigate the situation.

When you got a code red call, all you wanted to know was where to meet the caller. No time to ask questions, get your guns and meet me at so and so location, that's how we rolled.

Me and Mike were chillin' in our spot in the building across from DeeKay's. We raced downstairs to meet DeeKay and his right hand man Tony Reid. Arriving on the scene we immediately figured out what the red alert call was about seeing DeeKay with hand in his waist as he talked to Doe, and Tony holding his gun on the driver of the car that Doe drove to the projects in.

Approaching the DeeKay and Doe I could hear DeeKay telling Doe the candy shop was closed and the top half of the block was ours. Doe let out a sly laugh, something stickup kids probably practiced to exude confidence and cockiness. That's all Mike needed to get started, always a hair trigger away from exploding, Doe had no idea what he was up against. Three young drug dealers itching to put the exclamation point on the statement they already made to the projects and the stickup from Fort Greene. Before he could say another word, or make a cheap gangster gesture Mike already had pulled out the prettiest 38 special you ever seen, from under his jacket. Following suit in a split second Doe was staring down the barrels of three guns, DK's glistening blue steel 9 millimeter, and my chrome 380.

The look Doe had on his face now expressed his serious concern for the situation. Mike always the one to drive home a point, told Doe "don't take this personal" before smashing the barrel of his gun against Doe's face. Doe stumbles, almost falls and takes off running; we took off running after him. To get out of the projects Doe had to run through the projects, so can you imagine the scene where three black young males are chasing and shooting at another young black male, through the projects. This was the exclamation point that we knew would come one day, but we always thought it would be at the expense of a stickup kid from Fort Greene.

I unloaded my entire clip at the moving target, DK emptied his clip and Mike spent all his rounds and reloaded using the speed loader he carried with him anytime he carried his Betsy.

Eventually we had to flee when the sounds of the police sirens became louder, and flee we did. DeeKay cut through the alley between 111brigde St. and 177 Sands St. two project buildings, with me and Mike running into 177 Sands St. As fate would hRandy ave it DeeKayK got caught running into the 111 building and they confiscated his gun as well. The police brought DeeKay back to the crime scene where paramedics were working feverishly to save Doe's life. Looking for a death bed identification the police asked Doe was DeeKay one of the men who shot him. Not knowing whether he was going to live or die, Doe did something that would solidify his gangster in the streets forever. He looked up at my brother and said, "No, I never seen him in my life." A gangster to his heart, Doe sent word later while recouping in the hospital, "what started in the streets stays in the streets".

After the doe incident we pretty didn't have any major issues with stickup kids or other unscrupulous characters. We solidified our respect. We neither flaunted it nor took advantage of it. We knew it was there and that was it. We didn't get comfortable with it either, that could have proved fatal in the game we played. Thinking you had that much respect or fear on the streets that nobody would try you could get you dead. We stayed on guard at all times. Both DeeKay and Deb's spot and Mike and my spot were doing well. The money started rolling in. It was the end of 1988 and it seemed like things were getting better and better.

The better things got the more attention we got from the 'hood and the cops. I would say half the projects liked us and the other half despised us for various reasons.

We basked in the attention good or bad. As our reputations started to grow so did our status on the streets of Brooklyn.

When anyone mentioned getting money and Farragut projects in one sentence, the names you heard were DK, Mike, and Randy.

The brothers Antwaun and Shaun were the other half of the Farragut equation. They had the bottom half of the projects on smash.

In the relative short life of a drug dealer, I would have to say from 1986 – 1988 I was growing up in the drug world. I wouldn't become a grownup in the drug game until I began handling real amounts of money. The hustling we were doing in NY was nothing compared to what we'd do once we took our poisonous escapades to North Carolina.

Randy   Dee Kay   Mike

****

Money, especially illegal money corrupts many of men and they disregard the affects that their actions are having on other people.

During the time I was staking my claim in the drug world I was not only damaging my community I was damaging the relationship with my mother.

My mother; a very upstanding and respectful figure in the community was a teacher in the public school located within the projects. My mother didn't drink, smoke or hangout. She worked hard and was very much against the lifestyle that me and my brothers were living. She wouldn't take a dime from us. Because of me and my brothers' drug activity she would have her character called into question on many occasions, by her neighbors and her co-workers. Silently my mother had to shoulder the burden of her sons' illegal activity. A strong independent black woman I would later wonder how my mother dealt with the whispers and innuendo that surrounded her about her sons illegal activity.

My mother had to deal with the police coming on her job questioning her about the whereabouts of her sons. People were sending anonymous letters to my mom's job telling her principal about her sons illegal activity. On several occasions my mother had to stand by helpless while the police with arrest warrants in hand walked through her home looking for any signs of one of her sons. By no means was my mother soft either, she'd give the police a piece of her mind when they harassed her. They'd ask her if she knew where we were would she tell them, my mother response would be, "Hell No!"

Through it all my moms always maintained her dignity. But she was not happy about her sons being the talk of the projects in such a way that questioned her character.

It's one of those things that I regret to this day. Not only because I exposed my mother to such painful situations, but for also exposing her to the dangers of the drug trade indirectly. In an era where there were no rules governing the ethics of the drug trade, and with the chaos I was contributing to, it's a blessing that it never fell back on my mother.

It would take years and years to rebuild the damaged relationship between me and my mother. But my mother is one of those mothers that she loves all her children unconditionally. No matter how low I had fallen in life my mother has always been there for me.

My mother stood by me day for day since I was born, when I was at my worst and as I strived to be at my best. When I was running wild in the streets, she constantly tried to talk to me about getting my life together. She never gave up on me and never gave up on the belief that I would go on to do something positive with my life.

Today our relationship is the best it's ever been. I have given my mother something to be proud of and something to smile about when it comes to the things I am doing with my life now. I'm trying to replace some many years of tears with countless years of smiles.

****

It's November 1988 Mike gets a visit from an old family friend who lived in Greensboro NC. We'll call him Gee. Gee was a country boy who came to NY looking for someone to front him some drugs to take back to NC. Up until this point we have never even considered selling drugs outside of NY, let alone Down South. We did try something with Mike's uncle in SC but that turned to be a bad idea, his uncle unbeknownst to us was his best customer.

I remember clowning Gee about people in NC not even knowing what crack looked like and they really didn't. They were still buying small amounts of cocaine and cooking it up themselves to get high. The coke they were buying was trash so they never got the full extent of being high. When we introduced Gee to the real crack he was in awe. We fronted Gee a 3000 package of crack vials. When Gee left for his return to NC I told Mike we would never seen Gee again and that lost was coming out of his cut. Gee returned in 4 days with the 3000.00. We sent Gee back down with a 5000 package, Gee returned in 4 days with $5000. I started thinking Gee was either setting us up or he was sitting on a gold mine. I never really trusted Gee, anybody who smiles too much in the drug game isn't to be trusted and Gee kept a smile on his face. I always had been one of those people who like to look behind people's smile. The third trip Mike and I went down with Gee. We took $10,000 worth of crack with us.

Like I thought, Gee was sitting on a gold mine. What he failed to tell us though, was the same crack vial that was worth $5 dollars in NY was worth $20 dollars in NC. A 10 bag of dope was going for $40.00. Also my suspicions were confirmed about Gee, he wasn't to be trusted. He was smiling alright, making triple off the material we was fronting him.

Of course once Mike and I learned the lay of the land we pretty much moved our entire operation to NC. I guess you could've called us trail blazers, because we blazed a crack trail of mayhem and destruction throughout Greensboro NC, directly and indirectly. Me, Mike, and Gee were singlehandedly responsible for bringing the scourge of the crack epidemic to Greensboro, NC.

Our first full-fledged forays in NC consisted of what we dubbed The Family; Me, Mike, DK, Deb, and Gee. Things were going good. Two person teams would take turns going to Greensboro to oversee our interests and orchestrate things. Remember I told you I never trusted Gee from the beginning well if you observe a person closely enough and long enough you'll find things to fuel your initial perceptions of that person. The more I was around Gee and the more lil things started to happen I could see he was very sneaky.

From the onset I could tell Gee didn't want DK and Deb getting money in NC with us. I think he'd figured the less people the more money on his behalf. Gee seized on something that very few people outside of the immediate members of the family knew and ran with it. From the outside looking in you'd thought that DK and Mike were as close as me and Mike were, but that was just a front. They tolerated each other with phony smiles and fake love in part to keep the money flowing and the family persona intact.

Below the surface there was bad blood between the two. I would have to say that Mike was jealous of DeeKay, because DK possessed something that Mike was trying desperately to acquire; genuine love from the streets. The streets loved DeeKay, he was known and loved throughout Brooklyn and all the way Uptown in Harlem. DeeKay's name was ringing bells well before he started hustling, and hustling just heightened his street status. Mike on the other hand was plucked from obscurity and thrust to the spotlight because of hustling. Mike was thorough, he wouldn't think twice about putting work in, but he didn't have the same smooth style as DK no matter how much money we was getting.

So when it came to NC, Gee started putting shit in the game which eventually drove DeeKay and Deb out the picture. Gee not knowing how dangerous a game he played never knew his life was in danger. Me and DK hatched a plot to push his wig back in a seedy hotel somewhere in Brooklyn. But just as I didn't trust Gee he didn't trust me either and would never travel alone with me when he came to NY.

Things eventually blew over, DK and Deb would continue doing their thing in NY. Me and Mike eventually left NY hustling alone and put all our efforts into NC. Sometime later DK would also leave NY for another part of NC, Raleigh NC and blow up.

North Carolina was sweet. Less stress associated with the daily functions of running a drug empire.

We set up shop in a housing project in Greensboro called The Grove. For two and a half years we were the exclusive sellers in The Grove. We also had several workers, local and from NY selling in the open drug market called The Hill. Because Gee was from Greensboro, that opened the door for us to flood Greensboro with crack cocaine. We shied away from selling weight to the locals because that was the downfall of most drug dealers in Greensboro. We stayed under the radar for a long time because we didn't sell weight.

We'd send a whole kilo and a half of crack cut up for retail sale.

Things were good. Me and Mike would take turns going down south to oversee our drug operation and then sometimes we'd go down together. I played a very low profile while I was in NC. Unlike a lot of the New Yorkers who were making money in NC I didn't forget that I lived in New York. I was down there for one purpose and one purpose only to make money not friends. I didn't bring girls from NC to New York. I tell people anything about me, not my real name of nothing. I stayed in hotels instead of getting an apartment. If I had to leave town immediately I could pack my stuff in a minute and disappear instantly. My own workers from New York didn't know where to locate me at any given time.

Unlike Mike, I stayed out the limelight. His name had become well known throughout Greensboro and though few had actually dealt with him, he had slowly become somewhat of an urban legend. In New York, that's not a problem but in a small city like Greensboro that would be part of our undoing.

For a long time people in Greensboro thought Mike was the boss and I was his top lieutenant. Mike used to joke that when the shit hit the fan, he'd get life and I'd get less because everyone thought he was the boss. I used to tell him this was testament to the high profile he insisted on maintaining. Mike's name was associated with everything that went on in Greensboro from unsolved murders to torture of rival drug dealers.

I had no desire to make a name for myself in NC. The money we were getting in NC raised our status greatly in New York. When we went out we flaunted our drug world success. Sometimes we'd treat the whole crew to lavish dinners, throw lavish parties, and go on vacations.

We attended the events that would bring out the successful money getters in New York. We traveled and we traveled deep. When a good friend named Supreme from Cypress was killed we went to the funeral 20 gunmen deep; Me, DK, and Mike leading the pack.

One thing about New York was, regardless where you were getting your money from in the drug world, there was always someone lurking in the shadows looking to take what you got. Whether they could take stick you for a grip or they could take your spot, you always had to maintain your strength.

****

There are times that I think back and wonder how many dudes know how close they came to having their wig pushed back. How their lives laid in the balance of whether killing them would further a goal, make a statement or satisfy a beef. And on the same token how many times my life could have been held in someone else hands.

On the streets you begin to look at everything from the stand point of being tested. You try to read words, looks and body language. What lurks behind a smile or a joke? Something said in jest could have a far more ominous meaning. Mike used to say that I was paranoid. That I put too much thought behind others actions and I used to tell him everything is never what it seems.

Mike was clearly the reactionary type. Impulsive, ready to take it to anybody at anytime, and in the drug business that's a much needed quality but at the same time you need the ability to analyze things before you react. I was the opposite of Mike I was the thinker, always looking at things from every possible angle, going over things in my head over and over again.

True Story

Mike was dating a very attractive and popular girl from the East New York section of Brooklyn; this relationship would test the theory of reactionary tactics versus a thinking tactic on more than one ocassion.

A big drug dealer named Du from the East NY section of Brooklyn was sending roses to Mike's girlfriend (who'd later become his wife). She complained to Mike about the roses. Most people in Brooklyn knew that mike and his girlfriend were together, so this presented a question. Did Du know this was Mike's Girl? And if he did was he sending the roses as a disrespect? If he didn't know she was Mike's girl, once he learned she was, and he still continued to send the roses, then he was out right disrespecting Mike. Does Mike outright step to Du like he felt disrespected, or does he approach Du for an explanation?

After devising a strategy for approaching Du, we knew that the wrong answers by Du could lead to Du's demise right on the spot. The right answers could save him that day, but what he did after that could still be his demise. We also weighed in the fact that doing something to Du would definitely spark a bloody war throughout Brooklyn. But not approaching the situation could also be the undoing of the street status that we had so thoroughly built.

The day came. We knew we'd see Du at the Apollo Theatre on Wednesday night, because Wednesdays was amateur night at the Apollo and every known drug dealer in NY would go to the Apollo on Wednesday at least once a month. Du always traveled with two or three henchmen so we knew this could any way. We'd rather spark the drama then be booted out the exclusive club of ranking Brooklyn drug dealers for being perceived as soft.

Just before Mike approached Du we bumped into DeeKay. DeeKay was unaware of the unfolding drama, but he instinctively seen there was something afoot by the henchmen me and Mike had with us. Young gunners who were only deployed for the most serious of missions, dudes you rarely seen with us unless we are out to handle business.

DeeKay automatically fell into battle mode and though he and Du were extremely cool, one of DeeKay's famous line was, "If he gotta get it, he gotta get it." DeeKay had my back more so than Mike's because at the end of the day me and DeeKay was blood. And if sides were ever drawn against anybody, I would have always gone with my blood, which went without saying.

Mike approached Du, Du was oblivious to the situation unfolding around him even though he was at the center of it. Because Du knew DeeKay and Du knew me and Mike through Dee Kay, there was no need for Du to be alarmed when Mike pulled him aside. Me and Mike had a signal. If I seen Mike turn his baseball cap backward, then I would automatically shoot Du's henchmen right there on the spot. No questions no hesitation. This meant Du dissed Mike after Mike explained he didn't appreciate Du sending Mike's girl roses. This would be a defining moment in the long uphill climb in our criminal lives.

As he and Du casually walked down the block, me, DeeKay and Du's henchmen stayed at the top of the block talking idly. I kept my eye on Mike and Du. I don't believe Du was armed but I could be wrong. I know at least one of his henchmen was. Me, Mike and DeeKay were armed. Mike and Du talked for 10 minutes, which to me seemed like forever. Every sense in my body was on heightened alert, heart racing, blood pumping as I watched Mike like a hawk. At the end of the conversation that shook hands and I could see that the beef would not be cooked at least today. They walked back up the block laughing. Du gave DeeKay a pound and we all parted our way.

Blood wouldn't be shed today, and though I was ready to shed some, I was relieved that it didn't go down.

During this ugly period of black urban history so many young black men were killing one another and the affects can still be felt to this day. The mentality that drove us to edge of wanting or willing to take another's life is wrong. And it's only during my transition that I was able to tear myself away from that way of thinking.

Later Mike would tell me that Du said he didn't know that the girl was with Mike. And apologized, saying he meant no disrespect. That was all that was needed to avoid a serious situation.

This was just one of several potential situations that could have led me down a path that would have surpassed the destruction I was already spreading. I'm not proud of the life I used to live, but it was what it was. My mindset back then is the mindset that sends so many young black men to prison or the grave yard.

Pushed, I would have done whatever I had to do to defend the lifestyle that I was living. Selling drugs became my life. I woke up every day for the hustle. I would eat and sleep making my money. I was caught up in my own hype, feeling untouchable. At the peak of my street reign Mike and I had 30 people on the streets in three cities in NC.

Jail the journey that me become a Man

Breaking the Prison Habit

Book Review By Mumia Abu-Jamal

(This writer usually does reviews for political books, or ones which address the controversial or newsworthy events of the day. I will break that usual trend to review a book written, edited and self-published by a remarkable man: Randy Kearse, author of Changin' Your Game Plan.

This book will never be reviewed in the New York Review of Books, the New York Times Book Review, or the London Literary Review. And that's not only because it's self-published. The reason has more to do with the intended readers of this work: prisoners, especially Black men in prison.

Kearse writes to them, not to pontificate, nor to preach, but to share his own harrowing life story, and his climb out of the abyss, not merely of prison, but of the mindset that led him there, and which continues to lead others to the pits of hell.

He grew up in a good home, with parents who loved and cared for him, and did well in school (other than being bored to death). The lure of the streets called to him, and he answered, finding endless excitement, a lucrative (albeit short-lived) career in the (shall we say--unofficial pharmaceutical industry?)--drug dealing, which led him into a life of excess, of madness, and finally prison.

He tells the tale not just of his falling, but of his rise, his rebirth in prison, and his ability to question his earlier beliefs, which did not see him nor the vision he wanted to have of himself, his community, or the young who are to inherit this world.

In a series of essays, Kearse addresses issues of prison life and culture with a rawness and truth that can only be called refreshing.

I found myself reading things that I told friends just recently, in words that could've been my own.

In an essay called, Playing the so-called game, Kearse writes:
"We're the only culture on this planet that accepts prison as a [rite] of passage. We feel like we did something special when we come home from the jail house. We walk around like we accomplished something and that's not how it's supposed to be. We use the term 'I just came home,' like we were off on some world adventure." [p.44]

Years ago, while rapping with a young fellow who got caught up in the drug business, he began telling me about the hours he worked on the corner, or keeping his workers in line. I was, quite frankly, dumb-founded. He worked significantly harder than any "square" ever did; he told of pulling 20, or 40-hour shifts, stopping at home only to eat, or sometimes not even that. I thought of him, when I read Kearse's take on the incredible work ethic of drug dealers: "When we're on the streets doing our illegal grind we were workaholics to the fifth power. Sometimes we'd stay out on the block from sun up to sun down. We didn't wanna miss a dime. When we made it big in the drug trade, we put dudes out on the strip for us, from sun up to sun down. Sometimes we'd he hustlin' so hard we wouldn't even take a shower when we finally hit the crib. We'd get a call early in the morning and be right out. We put money in Front of everything and everyone." P.108

Kaarse's words reminded me of Huey P. Newton's observation that street hustlers and other assorted criminals were "illegitimate capitalists", who differed little from their counterparts working on Wall Street. Think of this: what's the difference between selling illegal drugs, and legal cigarettes? (To the consumer, not the vendor; for we know that one seller goes to jail, and the other goes to the penthouse.

Chanqin' Your Game Plan isn't a political book. Nor does it try to be. It is a motivational work, addressed to men and women who rarely have been directly addressed (at least with love). For this reason alone, it is worthy of regard.

There are quite a few youngsters, especially those doing their first bit, who will appreciate these words, for they will pull them back *from the brink of madness to the road less traveled--that of familial and communal caring, and yes, love. Kearse has said good-bye to "the game", and hopes, with this work, to encourage many others to do the same. With honesty and courage, he speaks to another way out from the dungeons.*

One hopes his work will find a receptive eye).

****

As a young man I never took going to jail seriously. I mean going to jail was an afterthought of what could happen if you got caught doing something wrong. Being young you didn't think you'd get caught until you got caught, and then jail became a reality. For me jail itself wasn't a deterrent, it was something that happened if I did something to get caught, so the name of the game I played was trying not to get caught. Think out, map out and then execute the criminal activity.

My first jail experience came at the age of 17. I had a long running feud with some guys from Queens NY, and it ended violently one cold November night at a roller skating rink in Queens NY. That night would change my life in more ways than I ever realized. I stabbed one of the guys that I had a beef with, he almost lost his life and I almost wound up spending the rest of my life behind bars. That fatal night, the guy I stabbed went to the hospital and I went to jail. He lay up in the hospital and I lay up in a jail cell. I would be connected to this person and the incident for many years to come, far after his wounds healed and I served the time for the crime. Even though I was charged as a youthful offender for the crime, as an adult every time I found myself in court facing a charge this incident would be brought up and ultimately have an effect on my criminal sentences.

I had heard the stories about the infamous Rikers Island Jail from the neighborhood gangsters who went and survived. It's sad when a young man equates being a man with being able to survive prison, but this is how it was. When you aspired to be known as a tough guy in the hood, you harbored the question in your mind whether when it was your turn would you able to hold your own in jail.

You heard about all the jail rules, the dos and don'ts from the older guys in the hood. You heard about being tried as soon as you walked in the door. You heard about the danger of being considered weak. What would happen if you left any challenge unanswered? You knew whatever happened on the Island definitely didn't stay on the Island. You knew when you stepped foot on Rikers Island, that you had to walk the walk. Talk was cheap and how your actions spoke for you.

The night I was arrested for the stabbing was the first time I had been locked up. I went through the whole process; for the prescient to night court, then the nerve wrecking dreaded bus ride to Rikers Island, it's like the line in a Wu Tang song, "handcuffed on the back of the bus, 40 of us, why life as a shorty gotta be so rough."

With all the stories you hear about Rikers Island, nothing can really prepare you for what's to come. You try your hardest not to look scared, but deep down the not knowing part is what really scares you. So on the bus you sit silently hoping that no one will notice you and maybe minding your business will get you through this. Too bad for me, that wouldn't be the case, my introduction to the world of Rikers would be a lot more noticeable. I was wearing brand new sneakers, a brand-new puma sweat suit, a black trench coat, an antique gold watch and pinky ring as well as four gold teeth; it wouldn't be so easy for me to blend in.

I still remember looking out the bus window as the bus made its way over the bridge that separates Rikers Island from the rest of the world. Going over that bridge gave me butterflies. With all the courage I could muster I pushed all fears aside and from that moment on vowed to never show fear. I stayed on Rikers Island 5 days before being bailed out, and needless to say I came home with every possession I went in with. I made it through and now I was a certified gangster. I had a few tests during my stay but nothing that I couldn't handle. My street reputation and the reputation of my brother carried me a long way. Not to mention that there were a few guys from my projects there helped as well.

When you really look at the bigger picture it's sad that as a young man I weighed the value of my worth on a scale of how I handled myself in jail.

I returned to the projects a bigger street figure then I left. I went to jail for stabbing a young Blackman and I survived jail. To the streets, I was building a reputation.

****

The stabbing case resulted in me doing 4 months on Rikers and five months on probation. I did the 4 months on Rikers Island without any real problems or drama, so I got out and planned to go on with my life. I had probation on my back so for a while that kept me straight. I was 19 years old now, I wasn't wildin' out or nothing, I was just going through life as most young people do thinking more about today then tomorrow.

I wouldn't see in the inside of a jail cell again until I started selling drugs. Only this time I wouldn't stay in jail 24 hrs after seeing a judge. On the rare occasions I was arrested I also had money to bail myself out. And If I didn't have all of it, best believe the balance would be there before I was shipped off to Rikers with all the so-called hustlers who couldn't make a 1,000, a 1,500 or even a 2,500 dollar bail. In those days your people could come bail you out cash money. I'd tell the processing person at the court don't waste his or her time doing my transfer paperwork cause I'm outta here. The sweetest words a jailed hustler could hear are your name and "On the Bailout" in the same sentence.

Never liking the inside of a jail cell I bailed out on a few cases knowing that if things didn't look good for me I was going to jump bail. I had accumulated quite a few cases in NY during my drug dealing tenure and those cases would eventually catch up to me. Not before I caught the big case; a federal indictment out of Greensboro NC.

There are times I wish I could turn back the hands of time, but we all know that's a foolish wish. I have my share of regrets. Having wasted a good portion of my life chasing an illusion it took me to be incarcerated to realize the street mentality will fill your head with all the glitter of fame, fortune and success but what the streets don't tell you is, the price you'll have to pay while trying to acquire these trappings. Some have paid with their lives or in prison for the better part of their lives.

Compared to Mike the outsider's fate and the fate of his wife I guess you can say that I got off light.

(I can remember the dreaded phone call like it was yesterday, I had been in Lewisburg a couple months, and it was March 1994. Calling home was my only window to the world. I was calling Denise the mother of my son. Her and I were going through some things and only having the phone to communicate with her put a strain on an already bad relationship. This particular day I called, she answered the phone and the first words that came out her mouth were, "I have some bad news". Automatically I thought this was the part that every incarcerated man fears, the day when the women they were involved with before getting locked up dropped the "I have someone else bomb". With all the courage I could muster I said "what kind of bad news?" She said, "Mike and his wife were found dead yesterday" "Both were found bound and gagged and shot behind the head execution style."

I couldn't believe the words that were coming through the phone, was this her idea of a cruel joke, then I knew she wouldn't play like this knowing the bond that me, Mike and wife had. Nah this is real. I would've rather had her tell me that she was sleeping with another man then hear the tragic news that she was giving me. This couldn't be. But it was. Mike and his wife were gone. Nothing would ever be the same for me.)

****

Even though I been to jail for several short stays, up until I received the 15 year federal prison sentence, the most I had ever spent behind bars was 8 months.

As a youngster I remember the long ride across the bridge to Rikers Island. Now as a man I'm sitting on a prison bound bus reminiscing about that bus ride looking out the window of a bus that will soon deposit me in the belly of the beast. Lewisburg federal prison would be my first stop. The Big House; Lewisburg housed America's worst of the worst federal prisoners.

As the bus neared its destination there was an eerie calm that took over the bus. No more idle chatter filled the air. No more boisterous claims of street bravado. Just a dead silence that pretty much said, "this is it, you wanted to play with the big dogs well now here's your chance".

As you drive up to the prison itself you can't help but notice it reminded you of an old evil castle. It was a dark, cold and dreary day I would arrive at Lewisburg, making the old evil castle look even that more ominous.

With so many thoughts running through my head, all I can remember now is praying to God that I made it through this experience sane and alive. Please God give me the strength to get through this.

Upon arriving at Lewisburg you have to go through a reception process, medical screening, mental evaluation, classification and then orientation before you can be cleared to go to general population. This process ran over a course of several days during which you were confined to a segregation cell for 23 hrs a day.

Once you were cleared for general population the only reason left for you not to go was, if you refused to go because you were too scared to go general population. One would have to say he was concerned about his safety and then the prison would place him in protective custody.

There was a ritual that followed once a number of new arrivals were cleared for general population. A prison guard would walk down the long row of cells and ask each cleared inmate whether he was going to population in a way for everyone on the row to hear. As the C.O. made his way down the galley to ask the "going out to population" question you could hear the C.O. call out the cell location and names of those who refused. They would be forever branded as cowards in whatever jail they wounded up after Lewisburg or worse "rats" people who have told on others. For those of us who decided to go population it would be our time to join the ranks of the worst of the worst criminals in America.

The day I was released from segregation I was given a bed role, assigned to a housing area, and told where to go. Your arrival to Lewisburg was already known from the time you hit the front gate. Your arrival to general population was anticipated from the time you arrived. Guys like me got a welcome bag: sneakers, soaps, shower shoes, etc from guys that came from your city, friends I had met in the county jail, and dudes I knew from the streets. But just as your friends knew you had arrived, if you had any enemies they would also know you arrived as well.

I wasn't in general population 24 hrs when I learned a couple enemies I had on the streets were also in Lewisburg. In this new environment rules dictated that enemies meet face to face immediately. And the rules also dictated that you went armed (with a knife) to such meetings. Respect and one's word was the law of this uncivilized environment. If you gave a man your word, you better be able to keep it. And that's how it was done.

My first meeting was with a dude named Bah from Fort Greene projects. Some years ago before I even started hustling Bah had shot my best friend A.D. while we were leaving a in Fort Greene. A shot that wasn't really meant for A.D., but because A.D. was trying to protect some friends from Bed sty from getting robbed by Bah and his band of thugs A.D. got shot during the melee. Me and A.D. were not being approached for robbery, but we couldn't stand by idly and let some dudes who were with us get robbed either. So we tossed the pass we were getting from the Fort Greene roughens and tried help the dudes that were with us.

Shots rang out and when the dust settled A.D. lay on the pavement with a gunshot wound. He was rushed to the hospital where he stayed for two weeks recovering from his wounds.

Fast forward several months ahead, and the scene is Bah in my projects, in my building visiting two girls. During the visit he's viciously attacked by two men wearing ski mask and wielding baseball bats. He's beaten within inches of his life. He barely survives. Word on the streets is Randy and A.D. were the faces behind the masks. After several months of denials, we say yeah we're the ski masked assailants and so what. I see Bah one time after the incident while walking downtown Brooklyn, he approaches me. I'm alone, he's with a couple friends, everyone appears to be strapped, we about to get it on right then and there in the middle of the biggest shopping area in Brooklyn, from nowhere my brother DeeKay appears, I'm not alone. He asks Bah what's really good, does he really wanna do this, Bah shows a sign of hesitancy. My brother tells Bah if anything happens to me that he's going kill him and his whole family. The whole family comment was thrown in just to put emphasis on the seriousness of what DeeKay was saying. As cold as my brother was known to be I knew he'd never go after innocents.

We all retreated to our neutral corners and the next time I would see Bah would be in the main Lewisburg recreation room. I know it was gonna be drama as soon as I heard he was there. But hey what better way to set the stage for my stay in the infamous Lewisburg federal prison.

The meeting was arranged by dudes from Brooklyn who either knew us or heard of us. Prison like many places throughout American society was based on tribalism. Brooklyn hung out with Brooklyn, Queens with Queens, NY with NY, DC with DC, etc. So this situation would be handled within the Brooklyn tribe.

Everyone at the meeting pretty much knew the history that warranted the meeting so there was no sugarcoating the facts. Being that Bah was the so-called victim it was his call how he wanted to handle the situation. I was just there to let things play out whichever way they would, I was down for anything. Me and Bah separated ourselves from the crowd and walked out of ear shot of anyone listening.

We talked about each incident, him shooting my best friend and him getting beat down. We decided what started in the streets stayed in the streets. We'd stay clear of each other while in Lewisburg and agreed to let the chips fall where they may when we got out. Fine with me, the chips could fall right then and there for all I cared. We didn't do any handshaking or anything like that, we just said our piece in front of the

Brooklyn tribe and that was the end of it. One thing about tribes when there's internal beef, there's always the possibility that the beef can tear apart the tribe when members of the tribe align themselves with the person they're loyal to. The last thing anyone from the Brooklyn tribe wanted was a Brooklyn on Brooklyn beef.

That out the way there was another not so major beef that needed to be dealt with. It was an extended beef between my brother and the brother of someone in Lewisburg. It could have been blown out of proportion but the brother of the brother my brother had beef with had his own problems to deal with without adding another situation like me on his plate. We saw each other in passing and just said that things would be handled between our respective brothers and that was that.

I wasn't in Lewisburg 48 hrs and I had already been tossed into prison politics. The next 48 hrs would prove to be even more dramatic. I had a Mexican bunk partner in the housing unit. I slept on the top bunk, he slept on the bottom. A veteran of the federal prison system unbeknownst to me he was a dope fiend and a member of the Texas Syndicate one of the most notorious Mexican gangs in the federal system alongside their main rivalry, the Mexican Mafia. New to the system I had never heard of both gangs and their blood thirsty rivalry. The mild mannered Mexican I bunked with never give me the impression that he was capable of the brutal murder that he and fellow gang member would commit on the fourth day I was in general population. This wasn't just a stabbing and then somebody died, this was a slaughter. I mean the two Texas Syndicate gang members butchered the Mexican Mafia member with swords that looked like they came straight out of an old school Chinese flick. And the cold icing on the cake was the murder took place at the entrance of the chow hall during the evening meal. I was in the mess hall when the slaughter took place and the police looked us in the mess hall for hours. The murder itself was a shock into the reality of where I was, but the other thing I found more shocking, was the pure disconcert of other inmates around me. Was I the only one who found the callousness of a murder within the prison scary? Was everyone pretending to be nonchalant about the murder or were they just as concerned as me? I wanted to talk about what just happened but nobody wanted to spend time discussing it at least openly.

This event would be one of the events that would shape me during the course of my incarceration. Later in the bid I would be in prisons that murders would occur and it would be then that I would understand how everyone was so disconnected from the wanton acts of violence, like I was now, after the first incident of murder in Lewisburg.

My short stay at Lewisburg was like taking a crash course in prison survival 101. You learn and you learn quickly about prison edicate, the unwritten rules of prison conduct and how to navigate the complex highway of multiple personalities confined in an environment made by men. You let your guard down for instant and there's no telling what can happen. I broke a cardinal rule during my stay in Lewisburg and wound up in an extremely dangerous situation. I allowed a couple guys to talk me into joining a basketball team. I had vowed to not participate in sports because of the tendency sports had to spark fights and violence. Against my better judgment I joined a team and during the third game an altercation broke out and I found myself smack dab in the middle of it. A teammate of mine beat up a member of the opposing team behind words passed during the heat of the basketball game and that fight set off a chain of events that spiraled out of control. Because the guy who got beat up was from DC and the guy who issued the beating was from NY it made matters worse.

DC and NY kept some type of beef going all throughout the federal system so the incident which started on the basketball spilled over to every corner of the jail. This was one of those instances when people from both sides of the rivalry wanted their side to come out looking like they were the stronger side.

If it wasn't so serious the game these grown men were playing it would have seemed utterly childish. By the time the incident got to the boiling point, two people had been stabbed and 20 people were thrown into solitary confinement. Eventually the twenty people found to be involved in the incident were shipped to various prisons throughout the federal system in an attempt to quell any potential violent confrontations in relation to the initial incident.

The lessons that I took from Lewisburg would help guide me as I traveled from prison to prison within the federal system. Never forgetting that the slightest misstep could earn you an early release from prison, but instead of going home you'd be going to the morgue. I took my situation serious. I didn't realize it until later on in my bid, how all the lessons I'd learned during my incarceration would help me when I made it back to society.

Randy and his mother, visiting room Lewisburg prison

Moms was there for me through it all

Change Your Game Plan: The Randy Kearse Interview

By Gary A. Johnson for www.blackmeninamerica.com

Randy Kearse is a very strong willed, talented and unique brother. Randy is the author of **"Slanguage" and "Changin' Your Game Plan."**

Randy was arrested when he was a teenager for attempted murder and sent to Rikers Island. After serving four month, Randy was released and tried to stay out of trouble. His Uncle arranged for him to get a good job in the garment district in New York.

About two years later Randy got caught up in the whirlwind of the crack epidemic. Randy was making fast money in the illegal drug trade. Randy was an above average student. He did his street homework and used his smarts and ascended to the higher ranks of known drug dealers from Brooklyn. With his partners in crime they hustled their way from the mean streets of Brooklyn to the too sweet and ripe state of North Carolina. At the height of his hustle Randy was part of a team of 25 "associates" spread across three cities.

In 1992 after a six-year run, Randy got comfortable, made a mistake and became a wanted man. The Drug Enforcement Agency (DEA), the New York Police Department (NYPD) and the Raleigh, NC, police were looking to bring him and his cohorts to justice for their "last dance."

Randy Kearse went to prison and served his time. He went to prison in his 20's and came out in his 40's. He is a different man, with a compelling and inspiring story. Last month, Randy stopped by the Black Men In America.com office and spent most of the day with us. This is a story that every brother should read.

BMIA.com: You served time in a federal prison. How much time did you serve and what did you do to get there?

Randy Kearse: I was sentenced to 15 years in Federal Prison. Being there's no parole in the Federal system I had to do 85% of that, which amounted to me doing 13 years 6 months and 2 days. I went to prison for a federal drug conspiracy. From 1986 up until I basically got caught, I had been trafficking narcotics from New York to North Carolina. In 1992 I was indicted, arrested and convicted.

BMIA.com: How old were you when you went to prison?

Randy Kearse: When I went to prison I was 27 years old.

BMIA.com: When you were serving time in prison, what did you do to pass the time?

Randy Kearse: I spent a lot of time thinking, and planning for my future. I read a lot. I'd read any and every newspaper I could get my hands on. I watched all the informative TV I could. I exercised and stayed to myself mostly.

BMIA.com: What was a typical day like for you?

Randy Kearse: A typical day for me would be getting up about 5:00 am in the morning and preparing for breakfast. By 6:00 a.m., I was out of my cell on my way to eat breakfast. In the federal eating breakfast isn't mandatory like it is in some other prisons. The job I had didn't call for me to get up early but I did anyway. I was looking forward to when I would be released. I knew when I got out prison I had to work so I got myself into the habit of "early to bed, early to rise." You can't accomplish too much lying in the bed half the day.

After breakfast I'd watch the news for about an hour and then return to my cell and straighten it up. It would be about 9am by now. I'd go downstairs and exercise for about an hour and a half. After exercising I'd go back to my cell take me a shower and prepare for the noon meal. During the down time I had waiting to go to the noon meal; I'd be reading or writing something. Sometimes I'd have a stack of newspapers that were a week old. After the noon meal I headed to the "office" (ha-ha-ha). That's what people used to say about me when they'd see me making my way across the prison compound to the library. Sometimes I'd go to the library at 9:00 am right after watching the news and skip exercising, but most times I'd be in the library right after the noon meal up until the jail had re-call.

BMIA.com: Re-call? What's recall?

Randy Kearse: Re-call is when the prison makes everyone return to their respective housing units so they can conduct a count of every inmate in the prison. Normally re-call is 3:30 pm. When we returned to the housing unit I'd watch the news until we had to go to our cells for the actual count. Once the count cleared I would go back downstairs to watch more news until the evening meal was called. The evening meal was normally called about 5:30 pm. Once I ate, I went to the job I had, which was ground maintenance where I was supposed to walk around picking up cigarette butts. Though this job was the lowest paying job in the prison, paying $5.00 dollars a month, it was the perfect job for individuals like me who really didn't want to work at all. We'd sign in at 6:00 pm and then we were sent off to pick up cigarette butts, but of course nobody ever did their job. Once you signed in you were basically on your own to do what you wanted until the time you had to sign back in at 8:45 pm. After signing in I would go back to the library or "the office."

I'd stay at the library until it was time to sign out. I spent a lot of time in the library for a few reason. One, because it was one of the few places you could go and think. The library and the chapel were the only places in the prison you could go and escape the madness that surrounded you. Most people who came to the library usually had something on their mind. There would be brothers trying to fight their cases, some writing books and others reading and going to school. You very rarely had any drama jumpin' off in the library. I had some typing skills so I'd make a little money typing for some guys.

Around 8:45 pm I signed checked out of the library and had to return to the housing unit for the evening head count. That count normally didn't clear until after 10:20pm. By that time I'd stay in my cell and read or write for the remainder of the night. Very rarely would I come out my cell after the evening count cleared. This was basically my routine for a large part of my incarceration. Let me add this, the reason I didn't want to work is I needed all my time to work on the plans I had for the future.

BMIA.com: So you your focus was on planning for life after prison?

Randy Kearse: Yes. I made it my business to stay connected to what was going on in society. There were guys who watched BET all day. Other would work out and play basketball. That was not the routine for me. The only thing that can help you when you get out is to prepare for the future when you get out of jail.

BMIA.com: What made you different?

Randy Kearse: I refused to let society write the last chapter of my life. I accepted responsibility for what I did wrong. I was guilty as charged and accepted that. Once I did that I was FREE to think about where I was going. Time is your life and you have plenty of time in prison.

BMIA.com: Tell us about some of the guys you met in prison.

Randy Kearse: You have a lot of smart guys in prison. Do you hear me? In my case, if I took the same energy that I used to beat the law into doing something positive, the sky is the limit. If criminals use the same work ethic in a positive way they can be successful in society.

BMIA.com: How did you get caught?

Randy Kearse: I got comfortable. I was doing the same thing for so long, that I just slipped up.

BMIA.com: We were talking about our young people and music before we started the interview. Share with our readers how you think young people have been sold an illusion.

Randy Kearse: Young people need to be aware. Young people are in trouble. It is our responsibility as older black men to show them the way. A lot of rappers are putting out a lot of negative images and selling our young people down the drain. Young people are in trouble. Rappers are talking about what he does from the safety of his studio and gets paid a million dollars. You go out and follow what he says and you get a million years. Think about it. Young people have bought into what rappers say the streets are about. I know what the streets are about. The streets are about NOTHING!

BMIA.com: Let's talk about your background. What kind of environment did you grow up in?

Randy Kearse: I grew up in Brooklyn, N.Y., came from a good home. Both parents at home, both worked. My mother was a schoolteacher, my Pops worked for transit. We lived in the projects but the projects I grew up in weren't buck wild. At that time most the guys I grew up with had their mother and father at home. All the parents worked. There's nothing in my background that could possibly attribute to the negative path that I took. I was an above average student all through school. I got bored with school and dropped out. Instead of going right, I chose to go left.

I received my GED without even studying for it. I went in, took the test and passed it 1-2-3. My parents instilled a lot of good values in me. They stressed education, making an honest living, respecting women, and things like that. They also did their best to show me that there was life outside of the projects so I had a good upbringing. The neighborhood I grew up in wasn't what most people would consider to be poverty stricken, so you can't attribute being surrounded by poverty to my decision to get involved in the drug trade.

People have this image of the brothers who choose to run the streets as coming from broken homes and growing up in poverty, when that's not the case for a lot of folks. Most brothers come from good homes even if they came from single parent households.

BMIA.com: What is it about you that made you say, "I'm going to turn my life around?"

Randy Kearse: For me, it wasn't saying **"I going to change my life around."** It was more like saying, **"I have to change my life around."** When you don't have nothing but time to think about your life, your past, your present and your future somewhere during those reflections you should be saying to yourself that you don't wanna spend the rest of your life living the life you've been living. When you're young and doing your dirt in the streets you tend not to think about getting old. You're out there running the streets caught up in your own hype, basking in the glow of being a ghetto celebrity so you're just living for the moment. Once all that comes to end and you're faced with the fact that you won't be getting out of prison until you're 40, 45 or 50 years old, reality sets in and you start thinking about what you're going to do with the rest of your life.

You know you can't get out and run the streets again, so in a way you're forced to change. If you can accept, embrace and grow with change you have a better chance of making it when you get out of prison. If you reject and deny that you have to change, more than likely you'll keep living the kind of lifestyle that leads to prison or worse, death. I seen so many elderly men in prison and I knew I didn't wanna spend the rest of my life incarcerated. The life I was living had taken its toll on me.

When it all came to an end I was financially broke and emotionally drained. I didn't wanna live like that again.

BMIA.com: What drives you to succeed and be the best?

Randy Kearse: What drives me to be my best is my desire to show society that I'm bigger than the stereotype they have for brothers like myself. Let society tell it, after spending 13 and half years in prison I can't come home and be successful. Statistics say that 78% of individuals released from prison return within three years. I come home to tear holes in that statistic. I'm on a mission to show all the people who stood by me and supported me during my incarceration that their support and sacrifices weren't in vain. Even in my darkest moments I had people still believing in me, so I owe them and payment for them is seeing me be the best I can possibly be. What also drives me is my desire to be an example for all the brother and sisters still locked up in the system. To show them that someone who came from where they are, still managed to come home and live a positive, productive and successful life. That's very important for me. I represent all the brothers and sisters who have to walk the road that I'm walking now.

BMIA.com: How would you assess your role and level of responsibility for the things that have happened in your life?

Randy Kearse: I only have myself to blame for the things that have happened in my life. I'm not one of those dudes who blame everything and everybody for going to prison. I did what I did. I was guilty. I broke the law. No matter how unfair that law may have been, when I chose to break it I left myself open to be treated anyway the system wanted to treat me. In life we all have choices, if you choose to make bad choices you can't cry foul when those choices come back and bite you in the butt. You have to take responsibility for making those bad choices and begin to make better choices. No one promised me the system was gonna treat me fair if I broke the law. Whatever role you play in a crime, once you consciously break a law whatever happens to you is of your own doing. One of the biggest problems people have when they're incarcerated is not taking responsibility for being there. In my book I speak about that.

BMIA.com: Who motivates and inspires you?

Randy Kearse: I'm deeply motivated by the memories of all the friends and love ones who've passed away. I lost a lot of good people while I was away. The memory of my brother Dee Kay who passed away in 2000 is a major source of motivational fuel for me. He'd never accept that I didn't rise to the occasion when it was time to rise up. Brothers like Malcolm X, Don King, and the actor Charles Dutton, brothers who spent time in prison and came home with a changed game plan, inspire me. Lesser-known individuals like Tony Reid, Kelvin 'Toast' Hopkins and Daniel 'Danny' Gonzalez who've kept their vow to stay out of prison also inspire me.

BMIA.com: Has serving time in prison changed your outlook on life? If so, how?

Randy Kearse: Doing time has definitely changed my outlook on life. While I was running around playing the so-called 'game', little did I realize that society wasn't playing games with me. It wasn't until I was behind bars did I truly realize the seriousness of my actions. Even if you take away the prison aspect of the lifestyle, how many times did I actually put my life on the line being in the drug trade? How many times do we hear stories about people being murdered in a drug deal gone wrong or during a robbery? Where is the 'game' in that? I have no idea. Doing time taught me how to appreciate what life truly has to offer. Time has a way of humbling you if you allow it to. I was able to put my priorities in order. I no longer take life for granted. My mother used to always tell me, "You get out of life what you put in to it." Your prison experience can be a stepping-stone or it can be a crutch. I chose the stepping-stone. I believe that regardless of what you go through you can overcome it if you want to. When you hit rock bottom you can stay there, or you can pick yourself up, dust yourself off and keep it moving.

BMIA.com: How long have you been out of prison?

Randy Kearse: I've been out 1 year 3 months in December and I'm loving it. (Ha-Ha-Ha).

BMIA.com: Did you find the transition difficult? If so, how so.

Randy Kearse: The first week or two I had to get my bearings but for the most part I fell right into the swing of things extremely quick. Within the first week I was surfing the Internet, had an e-mail address and preparing to self publish my first book. By the end of the second week I was employed so I didn't waste any time putting the plans I had into effect. I stayed abreast of everything that was going on in the world so I didn't come home still thinking it was 1992. Things like seeing everyone talking on cell phones tripped me out. I pretty much left prison prepared for the next part of life's journey. I came home on a mission. I had a solid family support system when I reached home so that also made the transition painless. I knew when I left prison what I had to do, so as soon as I got out I got right to it. I wouldn't say that my transition was hard at all. I didn't come home with all the prison mannerism, vernacular or pent up anger that a lot of people bring back to society so you would have never known I did time unless I shared that with you.

BMIA.com: What was the first thing you did when you got out of prison?

Randy Kearse: The very first thing I did when I walked into freedom was thank God for bringing me through my journey. I thanked him for giving me the strength to make the necessary changes in my life to lead a positive life. I went straight to see my mother and I gave her a long hug. After that we sat and talked for a long time. My mother has been my number one supporter and friend through my prison journey. Then she tried to make me eat one of her turkey burgers (Ha-ha-ha).

BMIA.com: Have you learned anything about yourself as a result of serving time in prison?

Randy Kearse: Yeah I learned I don't have a criminal bone left in my body (Ha-ha-ha). When the judge hit me in the head with those 15 years, he knocked the thug, the gangster and the street mentality right out of my head for real. I learned that I have the ability to bounce back from this experience if I believed in myself. I also learned that my prison experience doesn't define me, but it helps make me the man I am today.

BMIA.com: Do you have any advice for women and family members who are waiting on their man or their father to return home from prison?

Randy Kearse: Encourage and challenge your love one to create a vision for his future. Then encourage, challenge and support that vision as much as possible. Repeatedly ask him what his plans are when he gets out. Don't accept anything but a detailed plan. Show your love one tough love too. No one needs to be running around prison with three or four pairs of brand new sneakers. There's no need to send a love hundreds of your hard earned money so they can live comfortable in prison. The kind of support you give your love can handicap him, because you can make him so comfortable he might feel he doesn't have to change. He'll think if goes to prison again, he'll be just as comfortable as he was the first time. And lastly, be mindful of the reading material you send him, if all you send him is urban street novels how can you expect him to break away from that kind of mentality?

BMIA.com: Let's talk about your books. Tell us about **"Slanguage"** and **"Changin' Your Game Plan."**

Randy Kearse: **"Street Talk: Da Official Guide to Hip & Urban Slanguage,"** is not only a 700 plus page dictionary/guide that interprets the whole hip-hop and urban slang vernacular; it's also a documentation of the unique language that we as African-Americans use to communicate. I wanted to show the world that our language was more extensive then the couple of catchy words or phrases that make it into the mainstream.

Randy Kearse: **"Changin' Your Game Plan! How to use incarceration as a stepping stone for SUCCESS,"** is about the journey of change that one should embark on while locked up in order to come home and lead a positive, productive and successful life after prison. This is the blueprint for turning a negative situation into a positive opportunity. I've seen too many brothers return to prison because they refused to change their game plan.

BMIA.com: What do you want people to learn or get as a result of reading your books?

Randy Kearse: With **Street Talk** I just want people from our community to celebrate that we have a unique language. And I want mainstream America to respect that uniqueness. They'll get a hold of a word from our culture and run it into the hole and before you know it's like they invented the word or term.

*Bling bling is a prime example. With **Changin' Your Game Plan!** I want brothers and sisters to know that there's life after prison. Prepare for your future while you're away so you can have a future when you get out.*

BMIA.com: In your opinion what's the biggest challenge facing black men in America?

Randy Kearse: There are many challenges facing black men in America but if I had to pick the biggest challenge it would be breaking away from this 'street mentality' that has so many of us stagnant and unable to reach our full potential in life. That mentality that has us looking at the reckless lifestyle we live as 'the game.' That mentality that will make us kill one another over something as petty as a stare or bump. That mentality that says the only way to succeed is to sell drugs, the only way to get respect is to pick up a gun, and the only way to be a man is to bed as many women as we can. That mentality that makes us see women as nothing more than sexual objects and not to be respected. It's erasing that mentality to me that is black men's biggest challenge in this country.

BMIA.com: How can people reading this feature support you?

Randy Kearse: They can support me in two ways, of course by picking up both books, but more importantly by doing what they can do to teardown these negative images that society has of black people, in particularly black males. And one of the ways of doing that is being a positive example for others to follow. Get out in the community and talk to these young people, one on one or in a group, they need help.

BMIA.com: What advice would you give to someone who wants to follow their dream and turn their life around?

Randy Kearse: Don't be afraid to step away from the crowd. Being different is the true measure of a leader. Believe in yourself, in your vision and in your dreams even when no one else does. And remember, we all mistakes in life but it is what we learn from those mistakes and how we apply those lessons to our lives that help make us who we are.

BMIA.com: Anything else that you want to share that I haven't asked about?

Randy Kearse: One thing, if you have a friend or love one who's incarcerated, all it takes sometimes is an encouraging letter or card to set that person on the journey of change. You might not wanna deal with someone because they're in prison but these are the same people who will be returning to our communities one day, think about that. I can only wonder what life would have been like for me if my family and few friends had given up on me.

BMIA.com: Thank you for taking the time to answer these questions. If you have any questions for Randy you can hit him up at randykearse@yahoo.com or visit his web site for his book www.randykearse.com. Also check out Randy's other site My Prison Journal.com.

Randy Kearse: No, thank you for allowing me the opportunity to get my message out there. We need more people like you and media outlets like Black Men IN America.com to counter the negative images of our BLACK MEN IN AMERICA.

****

After the Lewisburg incident I was transferred to a federal prison in Indiana; Terre Haute federal prison. Just like Lewisburg, Terre Haute was equally as dangerous if not more. In this prison, gangs were the problem. Being from a city like New York where gangs weren't common, it took a while to understand the gang way of doing things. In Terre Haute New Yorkers pretty much banded together out of necessity. It didn't matter what part of New York you were from, those divides that were prevalent in Lewisburg were all but nonexistent in Terre Haute. From the time I arrived in Terre Haute I got the run down on how things went in this gang infested environment. New Yorkers didn't hang out together all the time but if someone from New York had a problem, New Yorkers all came together to find out what the problem was. Then we proceed to deal with the problem accordingly. Unlike Lewisburg, where Brooklyn hung out mostly with Brooklyn, the Bronx with the Bronx, and so on if you were from New York you represented for New York, even if you were from Buffalo New York. I caught on and caught on quick.

Being I was a stand up dude from Brooklyn I soon took on the role as one of the New Yorkers who people could go to get an issue resolved or dealt with. I didn't like the role but I knew that a person like me could handle the role. Dealing with this explosive mix of gang cultures you had to have people skills and that's a unique quality that I have always possessed. The three years I spent in Terre Haute was also a learning experience like Lewisburg was. There were four murders during my stay there and when I was finally okayed for a transfer back to the East Coast it felt like I was going home that's how happy I was to leave Terre Haute.

The New Yorkers coming to Terre Haute were coming younger and younger and they were hardheaded. They could care less about the delicate truces that were set up between New York and certain gangs. They didn't care about the boundaries. They didn't care about anything. Being young and reckless caused for a lot of bloodshed the last three months of my stay in Terre Haute. I was just glad to be leaving all the senseless violence. I was headed to the third maximum security prison in 5 years. Allenwood Federal prison would be my next stop, it was 1997.

When I in arrived in Allenwood I was pretty much a seasoned convict, so I didn't need to be given any courses in prison edicate or prison politics. I had developed my own blueprint to getting through the remaining 8 years and I wasn't going to allow these false prison manifestos to dictate how I lived my life while incarcerated or when I returned to society. I had become tired and weary of the prison and street mentalities. Mentalities that were in themselves screwed up. These mentalities always put emphasis on respect and principle but when you got to the core of these beliefs you could not help but to see the ignorance within these mentalities.

For instance, if you promise to buy a fellow inmate something from the commissary and didn't you could very well find yourself in a beef, if you and this weren't as cool as you thought you were. The inmate who didn't get the promised item can take offense that you gave your word and didn't come through on that promise. I've seen it happen.

One inmate's family is driving to come see him, he tries to arrange a ride for another inmates family member, the day of the visit the inmate family show up without the other inmate family member, the other inmate feels offended because his visit didn't come, there may very well be a problem between the two.

I have seen fights, stabbing, killings over words, unfulfilled promises, petty slights, perceived disrespect and other minor infractions. Things that would be shrugged off in the real world were blown outta proportion. This wasn't the mentality that I wanted to be a part of anymore. I knew this misguided thinking process was the crutch that I needed to get rid of. If I was to go on and do something better with my life I had to de-program and re-program my thoughts.

Allenwood was more laid back to be a maximum security prison. It was a newly built facility so it possessed more creature comforts than the other two ancient facilities; Lewisburg and Terre Haute were both 50 years old or more. So I guess when you make the savages comfortable you soothe their need for violence. Each housing unit had more than 6 color TV. You had microwaves, washers and dryers in each housing unit as well. The prison itself was designed to make feel like he could be living in a college village or at some retreat. It wasn't your typical prison design.

But with everything else if you look under the surface you still have the same nonsense that went on in every prison. I think when people don't have nothing but time on their hands and nothing positive on their minds you have a higher chance that that idle time will manifest itself in a negative fashion. If I had to say though the violence overall in Allenwood was nothing on the scale I had seen in Lewisburg and Terre Haute. Allenwood was a place that you could feel a little at ease. Violence happened and then it wouldn't happen again for a few months. There were two killings the whole time I was there.

Allenwood would be the place that I launched my writing career. I had been beating my head up against the wall trying to figure out what I would do once I got out prison. I had so many ideas. Allenwood would be the place that I ignited my drive and determination to overcome my circumstances. No matter how long it would take I was determined not to let prison be the end of my story. I was on a mission to re-define who I am. Prison was not going to define me, what I did while I was in prison was going to define me.

When I arrived at Allenwood there came a point that I stopped looking at myself as being locked up and starting looking at myself as being de-programmed. I started challenging my old way of thinking and started looking at the path that led me to be incarcerated. I think as time wore on, time itself started chipping away at the street mentality I had so proudly used for so long and started thinking about a better way of life. It would be up to me to take off the old set of street clothes and wear something different.

I don't know when the point came that I stopped looking at being in prison as being locked up and started looking at my situation as an opportunity to re-define who I am. I think it was a slow transition to that point. From Mike and his wife's murder to losing my Father and Sister to DK and Deb passing from the aids virus, I had been doing some serious soul searching over the years. It was like I was the last one left from the family.

When you lose people that mean the most to you, you are left to ponder your own mortality and what does life mean to you. I was fortunate in an unfortunate situation. Fortunate because I was still alive after all the madness I had been through and I was surviving the all the madness around me in prison. As I stood back and stock of my life I started to want something different.

Excerpted from Changin' Your Game Plan

(Over time I began to take a real hard and honest look at myself, my situation and my life. Slowly I started to realize that life wasn't over for me. In fact, life was just beginning again if I was willing to roll with making some serious and necessary changes. I began to look at my incarceration as a challenge. Did I have what it would take for me to reinvent myself, to make something positive come out of this negative situation? Could I do away with my old self-destructive thinking process and reckless behavior? Could I become a person that would garner respect amongst his peers and become a son a mother could be proud of? These were some of questions that I asked myself, the challenges that I set for myself.

With time and a whole lot of determination I set down the path of change and with change came growth, and with growth came a whole new outlook on life. A new clear sense of what was important in life and the ability to appreciate what life really had to offer came to light. While guys around me were still glorifying their misdeeds, reputations, and reckless lifestyles I was looking ahead. Instead of spending time talking about who I used to be, I concentrated on who I wanted to be and who I was striving to become. One of the first things I decided to do was let go of the past. My past had no room in the future.

It wasn't easy. Anyone who is doing time or has done time knows the struggles that go on in prison. I refused to let anything or anyone knock me off the course that I now set for myself. From my many years of incarceration I hope to impress upon you some of the lessons I've learned that lead me to do a positive and productive bid. One filled with growth, maturity, and a new found sense of peace. Doing time isn't easy, but how you choose to do your time will determine what kind of future lies ahead of you.)

It was during my stay at Allenwood that I started writing. I wouldn't realize it then but a simple conversation with a fellow inmate would be the turning point in my life that sent me down the long of success.

One evening a fellow inmate of mines had just finished a phone call with his young son. Most times inmates share the talks they have with family members as long as the talks were good. This particular inmate had devised a way to stay close to his young son. Each time he would call his son, he would tell his son a joke from a 1,001 Joke Book. I thought that was cool. After talking to the inmate I went back to my sell and being the entrepreneur that I am, I started thinking how people made money from 1,001 this and 1,001 that and started thinking what 1,001 book could I come up with. I wrecked my brain for several days. Then it hit me, 1,001 slang words. Hip-Hop was at its peak and I thought this would definitely be a winner. I started immediately.

What started out as a quick writing project turned into a project that would take 7 years to complete. In the end, I would have a 1,001 page manuscript titled Street Talk, with over 10,000 slang entries.

Writing went from being a leisurely way to pass time or a means to communicate with people on the outside to being a form of therapy that I used to relieve my stress. It became a vehicle in which I began to learn who I was, how I thought and why did I think that way.

This newly discovered gift was going to be my ticket back. A means to regain my dignity and self-respect; I became consumed with the writing project. I became obsessed with the publishing business. I knew I had a viable project in Street Talk and I was determined to get it out there to the world.

****

The Con's English How to write a dictionary in prison.
By Bryan Curtis
Posted Tuesday, May 1, 2007, at 7:21 AM ET

Listen to the MP3 audio version of this story here, or sign up for Slate's free daily podcast on iTunes.

Randy Kearse wrote Street Talk, his dictionary of urban slang, over a period beginning in October 1997 and ending on Aug. 17, 2005. Eight years might seem like a long time to nurture a manuscript, but not for Kearse, who was serving a term of 13 years, six months, and two days in various federal prisons for conspiracy to distribute narcotics. Prison was not a bad place to be a writer, Kearse said. There was plenty of down time and, as a lexicographer bent on chronicling the latest slang locutions, he had plenty of wisecracking muses. "Guys have nothing but time on their hands in prison," said Kearse. "So being able to talk witty, being able to talk slick, really highlights you as an individual." For instance, at the Federal Correctional Institution in Terre Haute, Ind., Kearse learned that if your cellmate has gone Viking—that is, he refuses to bathe—the phrase ain't no sharks in the water is a subtle way to convey to him that he might want to think about taking a shower. You know, when he has a moment. No rush.

Kearse self-published Street Talk shortly after his release in 2005 and later sold it to Barricade Books, a publisher in Fort Lee, N.J., which has brought it out in a handsome new edition that spans 700 pages, from a ass of life ("a large posterior") to zooted ("high on drugs"). The other afternoon, Kearse, who now works as a delivery man in Brooklyn, sat down over coffee to describe his unusual career trajectory. The hardest thing about assembling a slang dictionary in prison in the late 1990s, he said, was that the facilities Kearse was confined to didn't offer inmates access to computers or the Internet. Every afternoon, Kearse wrote on an electric typewriter and carried his rapidly growing manuscript, which measured about 8 inches high, back and forth from the prison library to his cell. When his fellow inmates saw him with papers under his arm, they would say, "He's going to the office." Whenever Kearse completed a few pages he was happy with, he mailed them to a friend in Brooklyn for safekeeping. Kearse has a round face and a big, inviting laugh, and as he recounted his story, he was clearly tickled by his entrepreneurial zeal. When he began Street Talk, he did not quite know what he was writing or whom he was writing for, but he knew he wanted to have something legal to sell when he got out of prison. Slang was his most marketable commodity.

Kearse originally set out to collate and define 1,001 slang words and phrases, a nice, round number which he figured would be enough to fill a book. Today, Street Talk includes more than 10,000 words and phrases, counting variants. Kearse has a keen eye and has taken care to make fine distinctions. Bump that can mean "to cut it out," but in another context it can mean "to turn up the volume on a song." He says foolery means "imitation jewelry," but foolio means "fool." Each entry in Street Talk includes an etymology ("old school" vs. "new school"; East Coast vs. West Coast) and a list of companion phrases or variants. For example:

tore up from the floor up adj. (e. coast slang) new school Unattractive; out of shape; haggard and unkempt; ugly. See also beat up from the feet up.

The most famous coiners of urban slang these days are rap and hip-hop artists, but during the Harlem Renaissance, the chief neologists were jazz musicians, the mainstays of the Cotton Club and Apollo Theater. Then, too, there were collectors of slang. Dan Burley, an African-American musician and newspaperman, jotted down some of the expressions in widest circulation and in 1944* brought out Dan Burley's Original Handbook of Harlem Jive. Burley defined hip cat as "a man that knows all the answers" and sadder than a map as "terrible, sad, disgusting." Cab Calloway, no stranger to Harlem jive, published his Hipster's Dictionary in 1944, and more recently there have been numerous New York-based slang guides: another volume called Street Talk! from a Harlem youth center; the Dictionary of Street Communication; and New York Addict Argot New and Old, to name a few.

Over the years, the word joint has proved to be one the most flexible words in urban slang. In Dan Burley's time, it usually meant "a club," as in "the joint is jumping." By 1961, Robert S. Gold, author of A Jazz Lexicon, added that joint could also mean "penis" or "marijuana cigarette." Kearse says joint has further proliferated and includes several new definitions in Street Talk. "Say for instance you say, 'Yo, go get my joint,' " Kearse said. "If you knew that trouble's brewing, you'd go get a gun. Now, joint could also mean your girlfriend, but it's pronounced joan. 'Yo, that's my little joan right there.' "In addition to marijuana, Kearse says joint now also refers to a kilo of cocaine. It could also indicate a favorite song ("That's my joint playing"), an automobile ("Is that your new joint?"), or a year in prison ("He got 13 and a half joints").

I found Street Talk so precise in its portrait of penal life—it read like a bleak, heartbreaking memoir—that I took a copy to Jesse Sheidlower, an editor-at-large of the Oxford English Dictionary and sometime Slate contributor, for a professional opinion. As a collector of slang guides, Sheidlower told me he prefers guides from amateurs who are collecting slang from their environs rather than dictionary professionals, who often pilfer from written sources. "I'm in the minority on this," he said. "But if I want you to get all the words for heroin that are out there, I want the ones you know. Not the ones you remember from reading Burroughs in college."

As he flipped through Street Talk, Sheidlower explained, "One of the typical things about self-edited books of this sort is that they'll include everything that is not standard English—slang terms, unusual pronunciations, a colloquial phrase that's not slang. But these"—he gestured at Street Talk—"are mostly real lexical phrases. The terms in here have a particular meaning, and they're used that way. Here's a good one."

[to] get a nut v. (sexual sl.) old & new school
1. to have an orgasm. (var. [to] get [one's] nut) See also: [to] bust a nut
ex. "Females wanna get a nut too, you know."

"With terms like this, the assumption is that they're only male," said Sheidlower. That Kearse had noticed female adoption of the phrase, he continued, was the kind of thing valued by dictionary professionals. Sheidlower flipped the pages.

[a] maytag n. (prison sl.) old school
1. one who washes other peoples clothes in prison out of fear or intimidation. 2. a follower; a flunky.
ex: "Ya man was my maytag in prison." "He lookin' for somebody to be his maytag." "They made 'em into a maytag."

Sheidlower said, "That's an insightful distinction"—one between merely being a flunky and being a flunky in a particularly demeaning way. "He omits the usage as one forced into sexual servitude, but let's assume he omitted that on purpose rather than that he didn't know it." Indeed, Sheidlower was somewhat disappointed at the lack of derogatory terms, but overall, he pronounced the guide "pretty good." He offered to submit some of Kearse's slang words for inclusion in the Oxford English Dictionary.

When I passed this news along to Kearse, he was selling copies of his book at a table on Church Street, between Chambers and Broadway. (Since the publication of Street Talk, Kearse has published a book called Changin' Your Game Plan: How To Use Your Incarceration as a Stepping Stone for Success and started a Web site for prisoners to post journal entries.) As we chatted, he said he was struck by how slang contains a lot of sadness—Viking sounds amusing until you are forced to spend 13 and a half years sleeping next to one, maytag sounds funny until you see someone humiliated into becoming one. During his confinement, putting a meaning to these words became a way for Kearse to hold his former life at some remove and, finally, to break with it. "I guess it made me realize that wasn't the life I wanted to live," he told me as he sold books. "I don't even use slang that much anymore, because I'm not into the things I used to be into.")

There were many people that tried to discourage me while I was writing. Other inmates would dismiss my efforts and laugh at my attempt to write a street lexicon. It was more them being jealous and afraid to do something different with their lives, then anything else.

I left Allenwood in late 1999 and I left with a completely different outlook on life. The road to reinventing my life, myself and my future started in Allenwood and it mold and prepare me the remaining five years I yet had to do. My security level dropped so the federal prison I went to was a medium security facility where I had a lot more freedom to concentrate on the things I wanted to do. I would spend 2 years in a federal prison in Estill SC. From there I would do the remaining time I had left about 4 years in a low security prison in Fort Dix NJ.

Doing federal time allowed me the opportunity to meet and talk to people from all over the world. The federal system was a mixture of many different nationals from every corner of the earth. When you sit down with someone who comes from a country where they have no real opportunities to do better and you learn how they live off of what we'd consider not enough to make it for a month, let alone a year, you begin to appreciate the opportunities that are available to you in spite of your past.

Excerpted From Changin' Your Game Plan

Learning to appreciate

(There are so many lessons to be learned during one's incarceration. Learning how to appreciate is another major lesson to be learned and to be lived by. When you're ripping and running in the streets you tend to take a lot of things for granted. It's only when you're taken away from those things and those things are no longer available to you, you realize what you've lost, thrown away, or neglected. Many times we take people for granted. Not taking into full consideration how our actions affect others. One of the worst things we take for granted is our freedom. We walk around with this misconception that we can get away with crime or that we're smart enough not to get caught without even realizing this is the way things are set up for us to think. To make us think we can get over.

To have gone through your incarceration and not learn appreciation is the same as going through life without ever learning what's important to you. If you're unable to learn these life's lessons during your incarceration, you're bound to repeat the same mistakes over and over again until one day you'll wake up an old and basically useless soul. No use to yourself because you've squandered so much of your life away and no good to anyone else because you haven't accumulated anything of value or substance.

Learning how to appreciate comes from recognizing your situation, no matter how grave could've been worse. It's also about being conscious that there is always someone in a worse situation then you're in. Learn how to appreciate the simple things life has to offer.

So many brothers fail to appreciate having complete control over their own life. They go right back to society and do the same things they were doing before coming to prison. Once you learn how to appreciate things like your freedom, make it a constant goal to never have your freedom taken away.

When you learn how to appreciate things, you hold those things dear to your heart. You wake up every day with appreciation.)

"Proper preparation prevents poor performance"

Mark Thompson

On The Rise Again

The part of my life's journey that took me through the experience of incarceration was a learning experience that provided me the necessary tools to face the challenges that I knew I would be faced with when I got back to society.

While I was incarcerated I drew strength and inspiration from other Black men who have been through and overcame similar struggles like me. Black men like Don King, the famous fight promoter, who was in prison for manslaughter. He served several years incarcerated, came home and became the world's biggest professional fight promoter. Malcolm X, who was once incarcerated and went on to become one of the greatest leaders of Black people. Great men like Nelson Mandela, who had endured many years of imprisonment only to get out and rise above their circumstance. Black men possess an inner strength that allow to come out of any situation greater then we went in. If we set out hearts and minds to doing something there is nothing and no one who can stop or deter us from that goal.

When I was released from prison all I had was the clothes on my back, a completed manuscript for Street Talk, not even a 1/3 completed manuscript for Changin' Your Game Plan, and a head full of hopes and dreams. Knowing that I couldn't live on hopes and dreams I set out immediately to build my life.

Excerpted from Changin' Your Game Plan

(Two weeks after his release he got a messenger job.... For a few reasons: to put a couple of dollars in his pockets, let his parole officer know he meant business and as a reason to travel around the city promoting his soon-to-be released self-published book STREET TALK.

In the first ten days of delivering messages he handed out 10,000 flyers for STREET TALK. He was able to finesse his way into the taping of the VH1 Hip-Hop Honors. He met reporters and celebrities, met rappers and other people while walking the streets of New York. He landed a college radio interview at WSOU 89.8, and did over the phone interview with an Indiana radio station. His book would receive book reviews in online magazines, newspapers and numerous people in the media would request review copies from the publishing company.

A major accomplishment would be the TV interview he did with Tyear Middleton the host and producer of tyeartv.com which aired on the Brooklyn Public Access station BCAT. What would signal Randy's positive comeback would be getting one of the oldest independent publishing companies in the country to buy the rights to STREET TALK.

While on his daily grind promoting STREET TALK he attended the Small Press Book Fair on Dec 3. Unable to afford a booth he just rolled up in the place 'hood style, a handful of flyers in one hand and a copy of the book in the other. Randy wasn't there 20 minutes before he was offered a traditional book publishing deal for STREET TALK by one of the three leading independent publishing companies in the United States, Barricade Books Inc. All of these things done within the first 90 days of his release from incarceration.

CHANGIN' YOUR GAME PLAN! is the second part of a well thought out plan conceived and crafted by a true Ultimate Hustler.

Randy Keys to SUCCESS

1. Patience… Nothing happens overnight. You have to allow time to pass while you're striving to accomplish your goals. I was forced to be patience while incarcerated, so I took that same approach when going after the things I want in life.

2. Attitude… Someone once said that success is 90 percent attitude and 10 percent aptitude. You're attitude can ultimately be what determines you success or failure in life. Poor attitude can almost assure that you will not succeed.

3. Perseverance… The strength and willingness to hang in there, even when nothing seems to be going your way, those who learn to persevere often succeed.

The race isn't always won by the fastest or the swiftest, but it is often won by those who can endure.

4. Plan… Have a plan A to Z. Most people don't include flexibility into their plans. No plan is foul proof, you have to give yourself room to mold the plan as you go along. And those who fail to plan, plan to fail.

5. Remain humble… Some people get cocky and high strung when things start going their way. Stay humble because you can get more out of your plan when you come across as someone pleasant to do business with.

Randy Kearse: Changing the game plan
By CYRIL JOSH BARKER
Amsterdam New Staff

Thirteen years, six months and two days. That's the time that author, motivational speaker and entrepreneur Randy Kearse spent in prison. And while most men consider time spent behind bars as a burden, upon returning to the outside world, Kearse considered his incarceration time as a steppingstone toward success.

Being out of prison for over two years now, Kearse is author of three books titled "Street Talk: Da Official Guide to Hip-Hop & Urban Slanguage," "The Writing Game: How to Print, Publish, Profit in the Book Industry," and "Changin' Your Game Plan: How to use incarceration as a stepping stone for SUCCESS." Numbers in sales for his work have reached in the thousands.

Who I am today is different than who I was yesterday," he said. "To understand who I am today, you have to know who I was yesterday."

Yesterday, meaning over 20 years ago when he was considered royalty during New York City's crack epidemic as a high ranking dealer. Kearse's previous lifestyle is a far cry from the life he leads today. With his books published and appearances at prisons and youth programs, he said he focuses on giving back and making amends with a society he helped bring down.

Growing up in Downtown Brooklyn's Farragut housing projects, Kearse said his childhood wasn't one typical of the making of a drug dealer. He came from a two-parent home; his mother was a school teacher and his father was a transit worker. Kearse was the middle of six children.

He said, "I had a decent upbringing, and no one would've suspected I would go down the wrong path. While I was in high school, I just did average teen mischief. I was trying to be cool and followed the crowd."

But trying to be cool led him to drop out of high school in the 10th grade, a move he calls his "worst mistake". He got a job working as a messenger and earned his GED, but at age 19 he was introduced to the crack selling business. Kearse recalls how crack ruined the lives of people during the mid-1980s but he had little concern. He was making $10,000 to $15,000 a day selling drugs in New York and in the South.

"Nobody really knew what crack was going to do at that time," he said. "On summer nights, it was like people were walking around like zombies. It was a terrible time. Nobody could've foreseen what was going to happen. Crack turned good people bad and bad people worse."

Kearse's drug dealing gave him a sense of power, he said, on top of the world. But that world soon came crashing down in 1992 when the feds, the DEA, and the NYPD and Raleigh Police came looking for him. He was busted in a hotel room during a drug raid.

He gave a guilty plea to prevent a lifelong prison sentence, and judge gave him 15 years. Kearse said going to prison was like going into a different world. But he used the time to get his life together and think about the future.

"My first three years [in prison] I was just trying to survive", he said. "I had to navigate the politics of prison. Six years in, I started thinking about my future. Prison is not about how much time you do, it's really about what you do with the time."

And with his time, he focused on being an author. Getting the idea from a fellow inmate, Kearse started writing his first book "Street Talk: Da Official Guide to Hip-Hop & Urban Slanguage," a dictionary of slang terms containing thousands of entries.

But it would be his second book – "Changin' Your Game Plan," a self help guide for people who have recently been released from prison and working to make the transition back into society – that would put him on the map. He also published "The Writing Game", a guide for aspiring authors.

Today, Kearse has his own publishing company, Positive Urban Literature Inc. He has brought his knowledge and wisdom back to the prisons by holding weekly workshops for youth inmates at Rikers Island and other places around the country.

"I took a lot away from people when I was living my old lifestyle. I want to take that influence I had and uplift people," he said. I hope to not be judged on the bad that I've done, but for the good I'm trying to do."

****

I didn't come home to play no games. As someone who had faced many challenges in his life already, I was extremely confident that I had what it took to not only merely put my life back together but put it together in a way that would restore my dignity and self respect. That's what all the preparation in prison was for.

I got a job, and had my first book self published in a matter of weeks of my release from prison. I had secured a traditional book deal ninety days after my release. I had been interviewed on radio shows across the country in as a little as six month from my release. My plans were slowly coming into fruition.

I released my second book Changin' Your Game Plan in Jan 2007 with great success. Doing things unorthodox, when I released "Changin' Your Game Plan" I released it straight to the street. No ISBN number, no bar code, no anything. Just had so many copies printed and took the book right to the street. I sold quite a few copies before I acquired an ISBN number and bar code, and with that move I launched Positive Urban Literature.

I went to a lawyer and had Positive Urban Literature incorporated. Everything I had done since getting out of prison had led to the day that I would start my own business. The feeling that I had that morning of the day that I would fill out the paperwork for my company is a feeling I will never forget. It was the same type of feeling I had on the morning of the day many years ago when I went to meet my first real drug connect. On the way to both meetings I knew after the meetings I would never be the same. I was taking a giant step that would change my life forever.

Sitting across from the attorney that would submit my incorporation package was one of the greatest feelings in the world. Only eighteen months prior to this meeting I was finishing up a 15 year prison sentence. It almost felt like I was dreaming. I knew I was on my way as long as I stayed focused and determined. After the formalities were through I went had lunch feeling extremely proud of myself.

Three weeks later, when my incorporation packet arrived, I got the same feeling that I had gotten when I had saved enough drug money to purchase my first kilo of cocaine. All my hard work, dedication and sacrifice had laid the foundation for this new venture.

I now apply the same drive, determination and passion I had for the streets and drug dealing to my legal business. I still have the same work ethics and principles that I had when I was standing on the corner or traveling across state lines to push that poison.

After everything I been through, learned and experienced in my life, starting my own company seemed like a natural thing to do. I knew if I wanted to really make my mark in life I had to do something that was going to give me a sense of independence. When you own your own business, you have the opportunity to do a lot more then you when you work for someone else.

Owning and operating your own business also comes with a lot of responsibility. I'm the author, publisher, publicist, sales person, account, and everything in between, but at the end of the day I'm my own boss, something I know a lot about.

****

Many of days JM and I walked the prison yard talking about the impact we'd have on the book industry. We never doubted ourselves. We come from a place that challenges us to rise above our circumstances. A lot of authors write the kind of stories that me and this brother have lived.

We have risked our lives and gave up our freedom in the quest to be known, to acquire riches and to taste the power of success. We foolishly thought there was a means to an end, but the end wasn't worth the means we applied to acquire success.

For me and JM, our writing is what helped secure our futures, but it's our stories that exemplify who we are. We are more than just authors; we are men who are leading lives that our peers, our children and our community can be proud of.

As JM and I planned our future from behind the cold steel fences topped with razor sharp barbwire, we vowed to use our experiences in a way that other Black men could learn from and be inspired from. That is our greatest mission. To motivate the brothers and sisters who come from the lifestyle that we have left behind to do something different with their lives.

As someone who used to be part of the problem within my community, I stand proudly today as someone who is contributing to the solutions within my community.

Me and JM have travel extensively up and down the East Coast speaking to young people about the perils and pitfalls of the streets.

****

Two years out of prison and I was doing a workshop with young people on Rikers Island. Once a week I would go to Rikers Island and teach a Changin' Your Game Plan Workshop. The course was 10 week course that went into the different aspects of changing the street mindset.

One day a week I would drive myself over the dreaded bridge that connected Rikers Island to the free world and every time I crossed that bridge I was reminded how far I had come in life. Once upon a time I would come across this same bridge in handcuffs shackled to the other unfortunate souls who had gotten arrested. And now 20 plus years later I would get security clearance to drive myself over the bridge. I would walk the same jail corridors I did as a youth as a grown man who had traveled a significant distant in life.

I would go into the Rikers Island jail to do my part; to do my best to reach a young black male before he gave his life to the system. If I don't go back and try to help the youth, then my journey is for nothing. I'm obligated to reach back wherever, whenever and however I can, because if I don't who will.

When you've lived the street lifestyle and have been blessed to have a second chance at life, it's your duty to help save another young brother's life. No matter how successful you become you never forget the struggles that you've had to endure.

Author afterthoughts…….

Life out here is no picnic. You have to work hard for what you want. You have to be willing to put in the time, exhibit the patience, demonstrate the discipline, use your wisdom, practice your humbleness, appreciate your blessings and most of all take your time.

It's been little over three years since my release from incarceration and I have accomplished a lot. I've had some setbacks, faced some obstacles and I'm still not where I want to be. Every day I strive to do my best, be my best, and give my best. All I came home with was a plan and a determination to succeed. I'm on the right track and nothing and no one will knock me off this track.

Changin' Your Game Plan, is the key to your successful transition back to society. Maintaining that game plan is the key to your future. Stay focused and diligent!

I went from being a foot messenger to buying my own van and becoming an independent contractor for a courier service. Now I'm starting my own publishing company, Positive Urban Literature Inc. to publish this book. I have many other projects in the pipe line.

The only people who are gonna make it out here are the ones who come home determined to stay out here. The one's who spent their time wisely, the ones who have a plan. There's a lot of opportunity out here. You can take these jewels I've given you and apply them to your life and to your situation or you can discard them. In the end it's your future and what you choose to make of it.

Next year my goal is purchase a piece of real-estate, do some traveling and continue nurturing my plans. Ultimately I plan to start my own Import and Export Company.

Never let your situation get the best of you. Only God and you control your destiny.

Since I've come home many people have asked me, what made me change my game plan. What was the single most motivating factor that made me embark on this journey of change...?

The answers lie throughout this book, but if I had to sum it all up in a few short words they it would be these...

I did not wanna return to prison! I didn't wanna give the system the power over me ever again! And most importantly, I didn't wanna take my mother through this ever again.

****
****

Being a black man in America is a challenge within itself. Being a Black man in America with a criminal background, no matter how long ago is a horse of a different color.

I had already faced the harsh reality of the challenges I would be faced with while I was in prison. I knew I would be dealing with issues from employment to housing. From being mistrusted by family and friends to the parole officer that I'd have to report to. I would have a scarlet's letter on my back for the world to see. If I couldn't navigate through the dicey waters of these challenges I would be shipwrecked on the shores of my past. Each challenge posed its own unique way of dealing with them. Some challenges you can anticipate and others you cannot.

When the challenge is facing you, you deal with it. You don't run from it, you don't hide from it.

Peace.

Randy Kearse

Changin' Your Game Plan: How to use incarceration as a stepping stone for SUCCESS

Available in Stores

ISBN: 978-0-9800974-0-5

MyPrisonJournal.Com, was created to provide individuals who are in prison an opportunity to be heard. A place where you have a voice. This unique media venue will allow you to speak to the world about issues that are important to you; prison issues, politics, relationships, sports, or whatever comes to mind.
MyPrisonJournal.Com is the only network of it's kind and gives you a monthly entry into your individual journal with a yearly membership. SASE to:

Positive Urban Literature Inc.
13 West 183rd Street #318
Bronx, NY 10453

Comments taken from www.randykearse.com/guestbook

Mike S. Sunday, 10/19/08, 5:57 PM

Hey Randy, Met you at northwest airlines ticket counter in atlanta a few weeks ago. You gave my co-worker Elaine a signed copy of changin your game plan. I borrowed the book and loved it. Inspirational as well as educational. One of my co-workers said that your book should be required reading while incarcerated. For those who really want a legit life I think that your book could turn them around. Of course all of us have cousins who see jail as home and when they get out it's just a short vacation to the old hood to visit friends and family then back to jail again. Hooray for you, good job and keep up the good work. Thanks, Mike S.

Email: gcingl

****

azaireyah Saturday, 10/18/08, 4:39 PM

dear randy your book is very strong and it is the best story i read in the world.

Email: azaireyahgatlin@yahoo.com

****

Pastor M.C. Palmer Friday, 9/12/08, 6:25 AM

Awesome by brother I am not sure how I got your information sent to me in an email, but I've just ordered your book "Changing your game plan" I plan to give it to my son who is in prison right now soon to be released. Your story is inspiring, just last Sunday I preached a sermon called "The positive effects of Trouble" and you are certainly living it. God Bless you.

****

Yvonne Ponce Wednesday, 8/27/08, 1:20 PM

Hello Mr. Kearse, I purchased one of your books at a 500 Men Summit held in New Life Cathedral, Brooklyn, and I find your book fascinating. I bought the book for a young man I know who is incarcerated hoping it would inspire him to stay focus. However, I started reading it as you suggested and I haven¿t sent it to him yet. I have to purchase another one for him because I am not parting with this book. This book was and is indeed a blessing to me and has further motivated me to strive harder at pursuing my own dream. I have never been incarcerated or even committed a crime. In fact, I am a Minister at New Life Cathedral and I could not put the book down. I feel your book is a tremendous blessing for anyone who has a dream. I was so inspired that I have been promoting the book to my colleagues, friends, family members and participants where I work. Hopefully one day you could speak to the group of young people at the church I attend or/and the students that attend the program where I work. Thanks & keep up the excellent work, Yvonne

Email:

****

Alberto O. Cappas Tuesday, 8/5/08, 8:03 AM

Please feel free to share "An Educational Pledge" with young people when you speak at schools and/or prisons. Keep up the good work. You prove once again that the key is to get out the box, to see the wonderful light in one's life and begin the journey guided by the positive light, directed by choices and decisions.... May God continue to bless your journey.... AN EDUCATIONAL

220 FROM INCARCERATION 2 INCORPORATION

PLEDGE I pledge to maintain a Healthy Mind and Body Staying away from the Vice of drugs I pledge always to try my Best to understand The importance of Knowledge and Education I pledge to paint a Positive picture of where I plan to be in the future Not allowing obstacles to stop the growth of my Plans I pledge to seek Answers to Questions, With the understanding that they Will lead to other discoveries I pledge to work Firm With the Awareness and Confidence That firm work Today will serve As the Seeds for my strong Tree tomorrow A Tree that no one will be able to tear down I pledge to learn proper languages, Beginning with my Mother's Always prepared to Appreciate others I pledge to gain a better understanding of Me By understanding my Cultural roots I pledge to fully accept Me as a human being A Rainbow of many cultures and colors I pledge to overcome any Personal misfortunes Becoming Stronger from such misfortunes Always striving to become A wise person.

Email:

****

juan ..."J" Tuesday, 6/17/08, 1:57 PM

Hello Mr. Randy , First and for most I want to hope your okay and everthing is on the positive and safe side. Mr.Randy you might not remember me ,but about three months of me being released I bought one of your books "Changing your game plan " while working my first job which was as a messenger..This was about early 2007. Well my reason for writing is to acknowlege and give you "props", because the book is excellent. I know it is 2008 now but never the less I've always wanted to do this....Stay strong

Email:

****

FROM INCARCERATION 2 INCORPORATION 221

THE GHOST OF THE PAST Monday, 3/24/08, 10:24 AM

HEY CERTAIN PARTS OF LIFE AREN'T FINISH.PLEASE BEWARE THEY'RE ARE SO MANY YOU AND OTHERS WHO WERE YOUR ASSOCIATES UNDERMINED?HOW WILL YOU MAKE A SPEEDY REPARATION FOR THOSE WHO AREN'T LIVING ANYMORE THEY'RE CHILDREN AND FAMILY,I FEEL IF YOU GUYS CAN PUT YOURSELF OUT HERE WE CAN REFLECT ALSO THE SAMEWAY.NOT ONLY AM I BITTER AT THE FACT THAT MANY PEOPLE TRY TO SWEEP THE PAST UNDER THE RUG BUT SOMETHINGS ARE STILL RELEVANT.I AM AWARE THERE ARE STILL PEOPLE IN PRISON BEHIND YOU AND YOUR OLD ASSOCIATES.I SEEN SOME OF YOUR OLD ASSOCIATES AT A CONVENTION IN MIAMI,THEN I SEE THE SAME GUY IN ATLANTA,HE ALSO SAID HIS LIFE HAD BEEN IN A BIND FOR SOME YEARS BEHIND THE PARTAKING OF THE CRACK EPIDEMIC THAT YOU GUYS WERE SO INVOLVE INTO.NOT ONLY DID I LOOSE A BROTHER IN RALEIGH TO THE DETRIMENTAL WAYS YOU GUYS BETRAYED BUT I LOST MY BEST FRIEND.NOW IM STUCK TRYING TO RAISE HIS DAUGHTER OUT IN THESE STREETS??TO BAD UR FRIEND WHO WAS BRUTALLY MURDERED CANNOT SEE WHAT LIFE HAVE TRANSPIRED UNTO AFTER THE COLD CRACK EPIDEMIC..

Email:

****
Jerome Livingston Wednesday, 3/19/08, 2:13 PM

  Bro. Randy, First I want to say I am proud of you and admire your determination, also a positive book "Changing the Game". Your book can change people lives, and provide hope also encouragement. I was searching for a PR and came accross Round the Box and seen your name. A few months ago I revised my book "Lust of a Dope Fiend" and had 1,000 books printed. I

222 FROM INCARCERATION 2 INCORPORATION

will be attending Harlem Book Fair and Brooklyn Book Fair. Randy you have a bless day and God bless you. Peace Jerome Livingston

****

deborah edwards Saturday, 3/15/08, 11:09 AM

Dear randy i happen to run across your book changin your game plan through a friend. my soon to be husband is now incarcerated not even knowing the out come of what he"s looking at.and as you should know that has to be one of the hardest part of your time not knowing when your coming home.i read alittle of the book before sending it to him and i couldnt get enough of it.i felt he would benefit from it more.he has called and couldt thank me enough.he told me that he has started incorpating some of your advise and knowlege into his everyday life there at the county.he said he did nothing but eat sleep and play cards daily but after reading the first three chapters of your book he now feels there is more he can be doing.he is now putting in for programs.i myself dont have a squeeky clean back round and want to thank you for given inspiration to myself and soon to be husband.at me being 40 and him being45 we can still learn.I WAS THINKING THAT MAYBE YOU SHOULD TRY TO GET YOUR BOOKS SOLD THROUGH COMMISARY THROUGHOUT THE PRISION SYSTEM.ANY AND EVERYONE CAN TAKE SOMTHING FROM YOUR BOOK AND USE IT IN A POSITIVE WAY.IF YOU HAVE ANYMORE LITITURE TO SHARE PLEASE LET ME KNOW THROUGH E-MAIL AND I WILL THEN GIVE YOU MY ADDRESS thank you deborah edwards

Email:

Acknowledgments

First I and foremost I thank God for giving me another chance to live my life, for giving me the courage and strength to embrace the journey of change and the opportunity to share that journey with others. As always I have to thank my mother Beverly Kearse, my number one supporter and best friend for her unconditional love. My friend from childhood to manhood, Ahmed (A.D) Dickerson for always being there to offer support and encouragement (and for reminding me that I need to pay back that hundred dollars). Jamal Kearse A.k.a Goobie, my big little brother (Thank you for giving me the opportunity to do what I'm doing. Not many people would have done what you did for me without wanting something in return. I love you. Sometimes family is family only until you need them for something). Tracy and Susan Kearse thank you for opening your door for me. Marguerite Spence, a friend to the end (always encouraging me to be the best I can possibly be). Danny Gonzalez, a friend whose new game plan is to be admired and learned from (thanks for being the real dude that you are). Aunt Jerry, Renee and Latoya Kearse thank you guys for everything that you have done for me, and most of all for believing in me.

A heartfelt acknowledgement goes to Anthony Smith Aka Heavy a true friend if there was ever one. If it wasn't for you I would not being doing the things that I'm doing now. I know I let you down but as I continue to navigate these sometimes rocky shores of life you are forever in my prays. You said it wasn't going to be easy and it hasn't been. Know that I hope to one day rebuild the bridge that I let crumble.

Thank you to all the family and friends who've showed me nothing but love and support. God Bless all of you.

IN LOVING MEMORY
Dennis (DeeKay) Kearse

Living in our heart and memories always!

www.ingramcontent.com/pod-product-compliance
Lightning Source LLC
Chambersburg PA
CBHW051823090426

42736CB00011B/1619